12/29/01
$25.50
dp

DATE DUE

THE LAW OF PRODUCT LIABILITY

2nd Edition

by
Margaret C. Jasper

Oceana's Legal Almanac Series
Law for the Layperson

2001
Oceana Publications, Inc.
Dobbs Ferry, New York

Library of Congress Control Number: 2001135846

ISBN: 0-379-11362-7

Oceana's Legal Almanac Series: Law for the Layperson
ISSN 1075-7376

©2001 by Oceana Publications, Inc.

Manufactured in the United States of America on acid-free paper.

To My Husband Chris

Your love and support
are my motivation and inspiration

-and-

In memory of my son, Jimmy

Table of Contents

CHAPTER 4:
THE CAUSES OF ACTION

CHAPTER 5:
COMMON DEFENSES TO PRODUCT LIABILITY CLAIMS

CHAPTER 6:
APPORTIONMENT OF LIABILITY

CHAPTER 7:
DAMAGES AND CLAIM RESOLUTION

CHAPTER 8:
TOBACCO PRODUCTS LIABILITY

CHAPTER 9:
PRODUCT LIABILITY IN THE MEDICAL SETTING

CHAPTER 10:
TOXIC TORTS

ABOUT THE AUTHOR

MARGARET C. JASPER is an attorney engaged in the general practice of law in South Salem, New York, concentrating in the areas of personal injury and entertainment law. Ms. Jasper holds a Juris Doctor degree from Pace University School of Law, White Plains, New York, is a member of the New York and Connecticut bars, and is certified to practice before the United States District Courts for the Southern and Eastern Districts of New York, the United States Court of Appeals for the Second Circuit, and the United States Supreme Court.

Ms. Jasper has been appointed to the panel of arbitrators of the American Arbitration Association and the law guardian panel for the Family Court of the State of New York, is a member of the Association of Trial Lawyers of America, and is a New York State licensed real estate broker and member of the Westchester County Board of Realtors, operating as Jasper Real Estate, in South Salem, New York. Margaret Jasper maintains a website at http://members.aol.com/JasperLaw.

Ms. Jasper is the author and general editor of the following legal almanacs: Juvenile Justice and Children's Law; Marriage and Divorce; Estate Planning; The Law of Contracts; The Law of Dispute Resolution; Law for the Small Business Owner; The Law of Personal Injury; Real Estate Law for the Homeowner and Broker; Everyday Legal Forms; Dictionary of Selected Legal Terms; The Law of Medical Malpractice; The Law of Product Liability; The Law of No-Fault Insurance; The Law of Immigration; The Law of Libel and Slander; The Law of Buying and Selling; Elder Law; The Right to Die; AIDS Law; The Law of Obscenity and Pornography; The Law of Child Custody; The Law of Debt Collection; Consumer Rights Law; Bankruptcy Law for the Individual Debtor; Victim's Rights Law; Animal Rights Law; Workers' Compensation Law; Employee Rights in the Workplace; Probate Law; Environmental Law; Labor Law; The Americans with Disabilities Act; The Law of Capital Punishment; Education Law; The Law of Violence Against Women; Landlord-Tenant Law; Insurance Law; Religion and the Law; Commercial Law; Motor Vehicle Law; Social Security Law; The Law of Drunk Driving; The Law of Speech and the First Amendment; Employment Discrimination Under Title VII; Hospital Liability Law; Home Mortgage Law Primer; Copyright Law; Patent Law; Trademark Law; Special Education Law; The Law of Attachment and Garnishment; Banks and their Customers; and Credit Cards and the Law.

INTRODUCTION

This legal almanac explores the area of law known generally as "product liability." Product liability law seeks to compensate a person who is injured by the normal use of a product. It is the area of law which polices the manner in which private industry safeguards the health and welfare of its consumers while attempting to maintain a competitive edge.

A product liability fact pattern generally involves a product, the maker, seller and purchaser of that product, and the person who has been harmed by the product. The injured plaintiff is not always the purchaser of the product. It is the product that forms the legal connection between the defendant and the plaintiff because the product is in some way defective.

This defective product, and the relationship among the parties who had contact with the product, forms the basis of the law of product liability.

A product liability case is somewhat of a hybrid cause of action in that one claim may set forth theories of strict product liability, negligence, and intentional tort—such as fraudulent misrepresentation. The governing law is derived from two main sources: common-law torts and the Uniform Commercial Code (the "UCC").

This almanac sets forth the elements necessary to prove the various theories of liability which support a prima facie product liability claim, the defenses to such claims, the responsible parties and apportionment of liability, and the damages recoverable.

This almanac also gives an overview of specific products liability topics including tobacco products, toxic torts, medical devices, pharmaceuticals and aviation liability.

The law discussed in this Almanac applies in most jurisdictions, and the applicable section of the Restatement of Torts and the Uniform Commercial Code is cited where helpful to a better understanding. Readers are cautioned, however, when researching a particular problem, not to rely on a general discussion of the law, but to always check the law of their own jurisdictions.

The Appendix provides sample documents, applicable statutes, and other pertinent information and data. The Glossary contains definitions of many of the terms used throughout the almanac.

CHAPTER 1:
THE HISTORY AND DEVELOPMENT OF PRODUCT LIABILITY LAW

PRODUCT LIABILITY—AN ANCIENT CONCEPT

"If a builder builds a house for a man and does not make its construction firm and the house which he has built collapses and causes the death of the owner of the house, that builder shall be put to death. If it causes the death of the son of the owner of the house, they shall put to death a son of that builder. If it causes the death of a slave of the owner of the house, he shall give to the owner of the house a slave of equal value. If it destroys property, he shall restore whatever it destroyed, and because he did not make the house which he built firm and it collapsed, he shall rebuild the house which collapsed at his own expense. If a builder builds a house for a man and does not make its construction meet the requirements and a wall falls in, that builder shall strengthen the wall at his own expense."

(The Code of Hammurabi, circa 2200 B.C.)

This is an excerpt from the Code of Hammurabi, the King of Babylon, who was credited with having established the first known set of laws in the year 2200 B.C. It clearly demonstrates that the concept of ensuring the safety of persons from shoddy workmanship is not a new one, although the remedies provided under modern-day law are not quite so harsh.

THE ENGLISH COMMON LAW

The English common law also dealt with its own concerns for the health and safety of its citizens. In grappling with these issues, statutes were enacted to protect the rights of buyers from negligent or unscrupulous manufacturers and sellers, the basis of such lawsuits being privity—a direct contractual relationship between the adversaries.

Under the privity doctrine, the buyer could only maintain an action against the seller, unless he or she had a direct contractual relationship with the manufacturer. The seller, in turn, could sue the manufacturer, with whom it had a direct contractual relationship. Of course, the "injured bystander" had absolutely no recourse under the privity doctrine.

Because much of our law is derived from the English common law, the privity doctrine found its way into our legal system.

EARLY AMERICAN JURISPRUDENCE

The two most important occurrences in the evolution of the law of product liability in America were the breakdown of the privity requirement, and the development of the doctrine of strict liability in tort.

The Breakdown of Privity

For many years, early American jurisprudence followed the English common law requirement that there must be privity of contract between parties to a cause of action. Thus, it was established law that a contractual party was not liable in either negligence or warranty to a non-contractual party. This rule of law effectively denied any recovery to injured third parties against the seller of defective products.

In the mid-1800's, an exception to the privity rule evolved which permitted recovery in the case of negligently labeled products. Shortly thereafter, recovery was permitted in the case of negligently made products which were considered to be imminently dangerous—a limited category of items.

This doctrine further evolved in 1916, with Judge Cardozo's ruling in *MacPherson v. Buick Motor Co.,* when liability was extended to a manufacturer of defective automobile wheels. The former limited category of imminently dangerous items was expanded to include items which would likely "place life and limb in danger" if negligently made—in this case, automobile wheels.

The requirement of privity in warranty cases similarly eroded, the courts finding no rational basis to differentiate warranty fact patterns from those underlying negligence claims.

The Introduction of Strict Tort Liability

In the 1960's, largely as a means to dispense with certain restrictions, such as notice of injury and privity, the doctrine of strict liability in tort was developed and expanded upon. Although strict liability was not a new concept, its effectiveness was previously severely limited due to the privity requirement. The doctrine of strict liability is more fully discussed in Chapter 4.

THE PRODUCT LIABILITY FAIRNESS ACT

In an attempt to provide uniformity and fairness in product liability law, Congress formulated a bill to enact the Product Liability Fairness Act (the "Act").

The text of the Product Liability Fairness Act is set forth at Appendix 1.

The reader must be cautioned not to rely on the Act as a reference for the law of any particular state, but to check the law of their own jurisdictions. However, perusing the Act can be helpful for a general understanding of product liability law.

CHAPTER 2:
THE SALE OF A DEFECTIVE PRODUCT

IN GENERAL

In its broadest application, product liability law deals with the placement of a defective product into the hands of the consumer by the seller of the product. This means that the product is unsatisfactory in some way when it reaches the consumer. Responsibility for the defect rests with all sellers of the product who are in the distribution chain, as more fully set forth in Chapter 3.

Generally stated, a product should meet the ordinary expectations of the consumer. For example, the ordinary consumer does not expect to find a metal screw in a beverage can. The presence of the screw would indicate that there is a defect in the manufacture of the product.

THE PRODUCT

The term "product" generally brings to mind a tangible item. Most product liability actions do involve tangible items. However, in the context of product liability law, this term has been expanded to include the intangible, such as electrical power delivered to a customer. The primary focus is an analysis of whether the defendant was in a position to prevent injury and spread the losses.

THE SALE

An important component of product liability is that there occurred a sale of the defective product. As set forth in the UCC §2-106(1), a sale is defined as the passing of title from the seller to the buyer for a price. As set forth below, the sale need not be to the plaintiff, as long as a sale of the product has taken place. In order for strict liability to apply, the sale must be made by a person in the context of the regular course of their business. Otherwise, the negligence standard would apply.

The Foreseeable Plaintiff

The injured person does not have to be the purchaser of the product in order to recover for injuries sustained. An exception exists in a minority of jurisdictions which require privity of contract to maintain a lawsuit for breach of warranty. The general rule merely requires that it is foreseeable the plaintiff could have been injured as a result of the defect, in order to recover damages.

Using the above example, a guest of the purchaser of the defective beverage can, if injured thereby, would have as much right as the purchaser to maintain a lawsuit against the manufacturer. It is reasonably foreseeable that the purchaser would offer his or her guest a drink.

The reasoning for this extension of liability is that a bystander should have as much right to recover damages as the purchaser or user of the product. In fact, the bystander is an absolutely innocent party to the occurrence, since the bystander had no control over the purchase or use of the product, and no opportunity to make an independent judgment concerning the safety of the product.

For example, Mr. Smith purchases a gas barbecue grill which has a defective tank. The first time Mr. Smith turns on the gas, there is a tremendous explosion. A spark from the explosion catches on the clothes of Ms. Guest, who is standing approximately 10 feet from the grill, causing her to sustain second degree burns to her back. Even though Ms. Guest did not purchase the grill, and was not using the grill at the time she sustained her injuries, it was certainly foreseeable that a person standing in the vicinity of the grill could be injured in the event of an explosion.

THE DEFECT

The key to recovery in every product liability lawsuit is determining that the product was supplied in a defective condition. The defect may be defined in a number of ways depending on the facts of the case. However, a defect generally refers to some problem, weakness, omission or error existing in the product which renders it unsafe.

It is not the mere fact that a defect exists which confers liability as long as the defect does not present an unreasonable danger. For example, a pack of gum may contain five sticks rather than six as the label states. This mislabeling is obviously a defect, however, it does not render the product unsafe.

On the other hand, certain products may be inherently dangerous, such as a nail gun, or a carving knife. However, the mere fact that these products have features which could cause serious injury does not make them defective.

Types of Defects

It is necessary to distinguish the type of defect so as to determine the standard of liability to be imposed—e.g. strict liability versus negligence—and, thus, the proof necessary to set forth a prima facie case. Defects generally fall into three categories: (a) manufacturing defects; (b) design defects; and (c) warning defects, as more fully explained below.

Manufacturing Defects

A manufacturing defect exists when the product does not conform to the manufacturer's own specifications. Thus, these cases are usually the simplest in which to prove the existence of a defect. The defect generally occurs randomly, such as in the scenario set forth above where the consumer found a metal screw in his beverage can.

Unlike other types of defects, when a manufacturing defect is found to be the cause of injury, the doctrine of strict liability is imposed, and the assessment of fault is generally irrelevant. This is so because fault is assumed when a product's manufacture so blatantly falls below ordinary consumer expectations.

Design Defects

Unlike a manufacturing defect, a design defect refers to a defect common to the product itself, and not occurring in a random sample. Thus, the defect is usually applicable to the whole line of products.

For example, a product may be designed defectively if it is found that it fails to perform safely according to ordinary consumer expectations. Further, a product may be deemed defectively designed if there was a cost-effective alternative design which would have prevented the risk of injury.

Although a design defect claim often requires a finding of negligence, strict liability may be imposed for an unreasonably dangerous design if the plaintiff is able to present evidence that there was a safer design available which was feasible to implement.

This standard of proof is greater than the mere showing that a safer design was possible. Further, there have been cases where a product was deemed unreasonably dangerous even though no safer design was available, in effect determining that the product should never have been manufactured in the first place.

Warning Defects

Warning defects usually involve some written communication accompanying the product. For example, a manufacturer of microwaveable foods may omit a warning on a microwave dinner that the outer packaging must be removed before it is placed in the microwave or it will burst into flames. This omission may be deemed a warning defect which, in effect, makes the product unreasonably dangerous.

Warning defects are often grouped together with design defects because warning defects share some of the same characteristics. For example, a warning defect, such as the omission in the foregoing example, also typically applies to a whole line of products rather than a random sample.

Misrepresentation

Products liability law may also apply even when the product itself contains no defect. For example, when there are misrepresentations, whether negligent or intentional, as to a product's capabilities, the misrepresentation would form the basis of the liability although the product itself may be without inherent defect.

Because the representation itself forms the basis of the consumer's expectation, the standard of implied ordinary consumer expectations is irrelevant. Thus, the "defect" is the misrepresentation. If the misrepresentation is fraudulently made, this claim would fall under the category of intentional torts, and is further discussed in Chapter 4.

Tests for Defectiveness

A variety of tests have been used by the courts to establish whether a product may be deemed defective. The most common tests for defectiveness are set forth below.

Ordinary Consumer Expectation

As set forth in the Restatement of Torts 2nd, §402A, the most common standard by which a product is deemed sold in a defective condition is when it is "dangerous to an extent beyond that which would be contemplated by the ordinary consumer who purchases it, with the ordinary knowledge common to the community as to its characteristics." For example, the ordinary consumer would not expect to find a metal screw in his or her beverage can.

The applicable section of the Restatement of Torts is set forth at Appendix 2.

Expert Testimony

The ordinary consumer expectation test for defectiveness does not work in all instances. The extent of a defect may not be within the realm of a layperson's knowledge, and expert testimony is then required to demonstrate the presence of a defect.

For example, if a swing set which claims to support the weight of a child up to 80 pounds collapses under the weight of a 50 pound child, expert testimony may be required to establish whether the metal used was sufficiently strong enough to withstand the weight represented. This evidence may be necessary whether the defect is one of design or manufacture.

Risk/Utility Analysis

Courts have also used other tests to determine the defectiveness of a product, including the risk/utility analysis. Under this test, an examination of the cost of making a particular product safer is weighed against the risk of injury present if safety measures are not implemented.

If it is deemed that the cost of safety is less than the risk of injury, then the benefit of changing the product to make it safer outweighs the cost, and the unchanged product is deemed defective.

On the other hand, if it is determined that the risk is minimal compared to the cost of changing the product, then the unchanged product would not be deemed defective.

For example, a match produces a flame which could cause a fire if it is carelessly tossed into a trash container. A plaintiff injured in such a scenario may argue that another design could have made the match safer insofar as they show that it is technologically possible to install a device in each match which would cause it to immediately extinguish when it is released.

However, the defendant manufacturer may argue that the cost of installing such a device in each match would cause the price of a book of matches to increase from 10 cents to $20.00. The plaintiff would likely lose this argument for defectiveness under the risk/utility analysis because the cost of changing the product far outweighs the risk of injury.

There are seven factors which are commonly considered by courts in their risk/utility analysis:

1. The usefulness and desirability of the product;

2. The likelihood and probable seriousness of injury from the product;

3. The availability of a substitute product that would meet the same need and not be as unsafe;

4. The manufacturer's ability to eliminate the danger without impairing usefulness or making the product too expensive;

5. The user's ability to avoid the danger;

6. The user's anticipated awareness of the danger; and

7. The feasibility on the part of the manufacturer of spreading the risk of loss by pricing or insurance.

The Unavoidably Unsafe Product

The unavoidably unsafe product is one which simply cannot be made safer given present knowledge or technology. Nevertheless, its usefulness outweighs its risks. This scenario is most often found in the area of drugs.

For example, there has been much controversy over certain childhood immunizations in that it has been alleged that children could have mild to severe reactions to the shots. On the other hand, if a child does not receive the immunizations, the risk to the child of contracting a serious disease, and the risk to the general public of unimmunized children spreading disease, is far greater than the risk of side effects from the immunization itself.

Thus, these immunizations would not be considered defective or unreasonably dangerous. However, it is incumbent upon the seller of such products to give proper warnings of the dangers and risks associated with the use of such products so that the consumer can make an informed decision.

When dealing with a defective product, it is important for the injured consumer to preserve the allegedly defective product in order to provide proof of the product's defect.

CHAPTER 3:
RESPONSIBLE PARTIES

IN GENERAL

Potential liability in a product liability action rests with all of the parties in the chain of distribution and marketing of the product. This generally includes the manufacturer—including the manufacturer of any defective component part—and the seller of the product. When investigating a product liability claim, it is important to identify all potentially responsible parties and gather all other information relevant to the case.

A product liability case information checklist is set forth at Appendix 3.

Also included in an action, if applicable to the facts, would be the assembler or installer, and the reseller in the case of a used or reconditioned product. Unless limited by state statute, others may be held liable if it is found that they in some way benefitted from the sale of the defective product. For example, liability could be extended to leasing and rental companies. In drug and medical device litigation, liability may also extend to the physician or medical provider.

THE MANUFACTURER

The manufacturer of the defective product is liable pursuant to all three primary theories of recovery, which include strict liability, negligence and breach of warranty. This rule applies not only to the manufacturer of the finished product, but to the manufacturer of any component of the finished product if that component was defective when it left the hands of the component manufacturer.

Product liability law no longer requires privity between the manufacturer and the plaintiff. The plaintiff must, however, be able to demonstrate a connection between the product and the manufacturer. A minority of jurisdictions still require privity of contract in a breach of warranty claim.

THE RETAILER

The Restatement of Torts 2nd, at §400, states:

> One who puts out as his own product a chattel manufactured by another
> is subject to the same liability as though he were the manufacturer.

Thus, under this section, strict liability would be available to an injured plaintiff against a retailer, who would otherwise not be strictly liable, when it sells a defective product. This rule would apply even if the seller lacked actual knowledge of the defect. An exclusion under this section applies if the actual manufacturer is clearly identified on the product.

This rule is a matter of public policy in that the public has a right to rely on the integrity of the seller, who is in a better position to put pressure on the manufacturer to provide safe products. Some jurisdictions have modified the general rule to exclude retailers under a strict liability theory when there is a solvent manufacturer who may be subject to suit in the jurisdiction.

Although all sellers in the distribution chain are theoretically liable, the retailer is not involved in the actual manufacturing of the product. Thus, it would be difficult to find the retailer negligent in the manufacture of the product. Nevertheless, if the retailer undertakes inspecting or assembling the product before it is sold, it may be found liable for failure to take reasonable care in the course of such assembly or inspection.

For example, a department store which sells bicycles in a boxed and unassembled state, direct from the manufacturer, would not likely be found negligent if there were a manufacturing defect in the bicycle. However, when the store offers to assemble a bicycle for a consumer as a condition of the sale, the store takes upon itself the duty to make sure that the bicycle is assembled correctly and inspected to make sure it is in safe and proper working order.

A sample product liability complaint based on this fact pattern is set forth at Appendix 4.

THE SELLER OF USED PRODUCTS

A person who engages in buying or selling used products is generally not susceptible to strict liability because the chain of distribution has been broken. However, if the used seller does something intrusive with the product prior to sale, he may be held liable under a theory of secondary manufacture if what he did caused the defective condition.

This rule generally applies only if the seller is engaged in the regular practice of manufacturing, distributing or selling products of the type in issue. Where the seller is not in the business of manufacturing or selling used products, but reconditions products for its own customers, it will not be held strictly liable, but may still be held liable for its own acts under a negligence theory.

THE ASSEMBLER OR INSTALLER

A perfectly intact product may become defective if it is assembled or installed incorrectly. In general, this would confer the same liability upon the assembler or installer as it does upon the manufacturer or seller of the product. However, where the product was already in a defective state before it reached the hands of the assembler or installer, courts differ as to their imposition of strict liability. Liability may turn on their ability to detect the defect during the assembly or installation.

THE PHYSICIAN OR MEDICAL PROVIDER

In the area of drug and medical device litigation, the physician or medical provider may be held liable on the basis that they, as "learned intermediaries," have a duty to inform the patient of the risks of the products prescribed. Complying with this obligation ensures that the patient receives the information he or she needs to make an informed decision about proceeding with the recommended course of therapy.

In general, the manufacturer relies on the physician or medical provider to adequately inform the patient based on the information given by the manufacturer to the physician concerning the particular drug or device. Of course, the manufacturer must supply the medical provider with adequate information on the known or foreseeable risks and hazards of the particular product. If it does not, it risks liability for its own negligence in providing inadequate warnings and instructions.

CHAPTER 4:
THE CAUSES OF ACTION

IN GENERAL

There are three main theories of liability which must be considered when bringing a product liability claim. They are (1) Strict Liability; (2) Negligence; and (3) Breach of Warranty.

Another theory of liability which may apply in certain limited fact patterns is fraudulent misrepresentation, which would fall under the category of intentional torts. These theories of liability are discussed below.

STRICT LIABILITY

In General

Strict liability refers to the liability in tort of manufacturers, for harm caused by their defective products, without any necessity for the plaintiff to prove fault on the part of the manufacturer. This elimination of fault was a monumental victory for consumers because it was often difficult to meet the fault standard of proof although the underlying claim was justified.

Further, the consumer is not in a position to detect a defect, nor should he or she bear the burden imposed when an injury results. It is the marketers of the product who are best able to bear the financial responsibility for injuries caused by their defective products, and adjust their costs accordingly.

Thus, under strict liability, the issues are product-oriented. For example: Does the *product* meet the manufacturer's own specifications? Does the *product* provide adequate warnings? Does the *product's* design render it unsafe in comparison to the design of other comparable products?

This straightforward analysis of strict liability provides a clear guideline for the trier of fact to decide the issues. There is no concern for the good or evil intentions of the manufacturer. Their analysis must simply focus on the acceptable legal standard for such a product, and the defect which made this product unreasonably dangerous compared to that standard.

The minority concurring opinion of Justice Traynor in a 1944 case, *Escola v. Coca-Cola Bottling Company*, is noted to be the origin of this strict liability reasoning, as demonstrated by the following excerpt from that opinion:

> *"I believe the manufacturer's negligence should no longer be singled out as the basis of a plaintiff's right to recover in cases like the present one. In my opinion, it should now be recognized that a manufacturer incurs an absolute liability when an article that he has placed on the market, knowing that it is to be used without inspection, proves to have a defect that causes injury . . . [I]t is evident that the manufacturer can anticipate some hazards and guard against the recurrence of others, as the public cannot . . . [T]he risk of injury can be insured by the manufacturer and distributed among the public as a cost of doing business . . . [I]t is to the public interest to place the responsibility for whatever injury [the defective products] may cause upon the manufacturer, who, even if he is not negligent in the manufacture of the product, is responsible for its reaching the market."*

The Prima Facie Case

In order for a plaintiff to recover on a strict liability theory, he must prove the following elements:

1. The defendant is engaged in the business of manufacturing, selling, distributing or supplying the product, or engaged in the business of renting or leasing the product. It should be noted, however, that some state statutes have restricted the application of strict liability to manufacturers, and readers are cautioned to check the law of their own jurisdictions on this matter.

2. The product contained a condition that was unreasonably dangerous. To be unreasonably dangerous, one must show that the product was dangerous to an extent beyond that which would be contemplated by the ordinary consumer. A more complete discussion of what constitutes a defect can be found in Chapter 2.

3. The condition existed at the time it left the defendant's control. The defendant will not be liable for a defect caused by the subsequent mishandling of a product which left its control in an acceptable condition.

4. The plaintiff sustained injury.

5. The unreasonably dangerous condition of the product was a proximate cause of the injury.

NEGLIGENCE

In General

There are certain advantages, both to the plaintiff and defendant, when a negligence claim is included in a product liability lawsuit, even where the strict liability remedy is also available.

As a strategic tactic, inclusion of a negligence claim permits the plaintiff access, through discovery, to certain evidence that would be irrelevant in a strict liability case. Further, a jury may be more prone to award a higher amount when the defendant's carelessness is clearly demonstrated, whereas fault is irrelevant in a strict liability case.

On the other hand, a defendant may welcome the negligence claim because it permits the introduction of self-serving evidence which may demonstrate the defendant's due care and diligence, such as extensive product testing records. Further, a claim of negligence brings into play the contributory fault of the plaintiff, which may serve to significantly reduce a jury verdict.

Thus, unlike the strict liability claim, an analysis of the issues in a negligence claim are conduct-oriented rather than product-oriented.

For example: Did the manufacturer adequately test the product before it was placed on the market? Did the manufacturer unreasonably cut corners when it chose to use a lower-grade metal which was more cost-efficient but produced a weaker foundation in a product?

These are the types of issues which are presented to the jury in determining whether the conduct of the defendant was negligent.

The Prima Facie Case

Negligence encompasses unintentionally caused harms, and is the most important basis of tort liability in the United States. The basis of liability is the creation of an unreasonable risk of harm to another.

In a product liability action, a defendant who manufactures a product which causes injury is not held liable in negligence simply because there was some risk of injury. If this were the case, then every manufacturer of carving knives would soon be out of business.

For negligence to be found, the product must involve a risk of harm greater than society is willing to accept in light of the benefits to be derived from that product—an unreasonable danger.

To prove negligence in a product liability case, one must establish that there was:

(a) a duty of care owed by the defendant to the plaintiff;

(b) a breach of that duty;

(c) proximate cause that the breach of the duty caused injury to the plaintiff in a direct and natural sequence; and

(d) injury to the plaintiff.

Duty

The duty owed by the manufacturer and seller of a product to the consumer is the exercise of a certain standard of care in the design, manufacture and distribution of the product.

The reasonableness of the defendant's conduct in its relationship to the product is key, even moreso than the defect itself. If the defendant had acted reasonably in all aspects of the design and manufacture of the product, it is less likely that the defect and resulting injury would have occurred.

Breach of Duty

There has been a breach by the manufacturer or seller of its duty of care if it has done something, or failed to do something, thereby causing an unreasonable risk of danger to another. That act or omission is measured against the conduct of the "reasonably prudent" manufacturer or seller given the same situation, and whether it would have anticipated the harm and taken some action to avoid it.

For example, in the previous fact pattern set forth in Chapter 2, the defendant failed to include a warning on a microwave dinner which would instruct the consumer to remove the outer packaging before placing it in the microwave. The plaintiff was injured when the dinner burst into flames.

The prudent manufacturer, knowing that failure to remove this outer packaging could cause a fire, would certainly include a very clear and prominent warning on the outer packaging. The prudent manufacturer may even elect to use a different material which would not cause a fire if it was mistakenly placed in the microwave.

In either case, measuring the defendant's conduct against that of the prudent manufacturer, the defendant's omission clearly caused an unreasonable risk of harm to the consumer and was thus negligent.

The proof of breach of duty of care is usually established through the use of expert testimony. Expert witnesses are asked questions requiring testimony that is beyond lay knowledge. If the information is highly technical, expert witnesses are permitted to draw a conclusion. However, concerning matters which the jury can understand, an expert witness is not permitted to draw his legal conclusion or opinion and render it to the jury.

Proximate Cause

The plaintiff must further prove the causal relationship between the defendant's negligence and the resulting defective product, and the injury sustained by the plaintiff. In this respect, it is crucial to preserve the product or its remains for testing and investigation.

Negligence Per Se

In certain cases, the violation of a federal or state regulatory or statutory requirement concerning product quality may invoke the doctrine of negligence per se. In determining whether the violation of a statute or regulation may be applied as proof of negligence, there are two questions which should be asked:

(1) Is the injured person within the class of persons who are protected by statute from suffering a certain injury? and

(2) Is the particular injury the statute seeks to prevent the same injury the plaintiff has suffered?

If the answer to both questions is yes, then the violation of that statute may be introduced as evidence of negligence.

The Doctrine of Res Ipsa Loquitur

"Res Ipsa Loquitur" is Latin for "the thing speaks for itself." This doctrine allows a plaintiff to be victorious in certain cases when there is a gap in the evidence which prevents the plaintiff from proving the defendant's specific negligent conduct. Most states permit, but do not compel, an inference of negligence in such a case.

There are two foundations for application of the doctrine of res ipsa loquitur:

(1) There must be exclusive control and management by the defendant of the instrument which caused the injury, and the plaintiff must not have contributed to the accident.

(2) The accident could not have happened without the absence of due care by the defendant.

For example, if the plaintiff purchased a can of soda from the grocer and, upon opening it, discovered a rabbit's foot inside, (a) the product was in its original unopened container at the time of the discovery, and (b) the presence of a rabbit's foot in the beverage could not have occurred without the absence of due care.

However, if the plaintiff is able to allege specific negligent acts, the doctrine of res ipsa loquitur would not apply. Further, the defendant is permitted to rebut the inference of negligence by showing that he exercised due care.

BREACH OF WARRANTY

Breach of warranty is a claim which sounds in contract rather than tort. As such, this claim offers a significantly longer statute of limitations than does a tort action. This should be a consideration when a claim has been presented for which the applicable tort statute of limitations has expired.

There are three types of warranties upon which a consumer relies which may be violated: (1) Express Warranty; (2) Implied Warranty of Merchantability; and (3) Implied Warranty of Fitness for a Particular Purpose.

It is quite common to include all three breach of warranty claims in one action, provided that the plaintiff can meet his or her burden of proof as to the evidentiary requirements. A description of each claim and the necessary elements to prove a prima facie case are set forth below.

Express Warranty

An express warranty includes oral or written promises by the seller that the product will perform in a certain manner, or that the product conforms to its description.

According to Section 2-313 of the Uniform Commercial Code (UCC), an express warranty is any affirmation of fact, description or sample furnished by the seller to the buyer that relates to the goods and becomes part of the basis of the bargain. Thus, it is expressly warranted that the product will conform to such affirmation, description or sample.

Further, it is not necessary that the warranty be reduced to writing, nor that any particular words be used, such as "guarantee," in order to create the obligation, as long as the representations were meant to be factual and not mere opinion. A thorough search of all product-related advertising, packaging and promotional items should be accomplished to either (a) uncover and demonstrate the warranty in the case of the plaintiff, or (b) in the case of the defendant, to show that there were no express warranties concerning the product.

The Prima Facie Case

In pursuing a claim under breach of express warranty, the burden of proof lies with the plaintiff to establish that:

1. The defendant made an express representation relative to the defective feature of the product;

2. The plaintiff knew about the representation; and

3. The plaintiff relied on the representation to his or her detriment.

Depending on the jurisdiction, local statutes may have additional requirements, e.g., timely notice of the breach to the defendant.

Implied Warranty of Merchantability

An implied warranty of merchantability is an implied representation that the product is free of defects and meets the general standards of acceptability.

For example, a pair of shoes should last for more than one week. If they fall apart before that time, with normal use, they are unacceptable.

According to Section 2-316 of the Uniform Commercial Code (UCC), a warranty of merchantability is implied in a contract of sale if the seller is considered a merchant in goods of that type, unless the implied warranty is excluded or modified. Under this section, merchantable goods are those which:

1. Pass without objection in the trade;

2. Are of fair average quality;

3. Are fit for the ordinary purposes for which such goods are used;

4. Are of uniform kind, quality, and quantity within each unit or shipment;

5. Are adequately contained, packaged, and labeled; and

6. Conform to any express warranty given on the container or label.

Because a breach of implied warranty of merchantability results in an unacceptable product, it is unnecessary to prove reliance by the customer on either express or implied representations of the defendant. The unacceptable product itself forms the basis of the breach.

The Prima Facie Case

In pursuing a claim under breach of implied warranty of merchantability, the burden of proof lies with the plaintiff to establish the following elements:

1. There must be a sale or other surrender of the product for some type of consideration, such as a lease.

2. The defendant must be a dealer in goods of that type in the regular course of his or her business.

3. There must be a defect, such as a design, manufacturing, or warning defect, which renders the product unsuitable for its ordinary purpose.

Depending on the jurisdiction, local statutes may have additional requirements, e.g., timely notice of the product defect to the defendant.

Implied Warranty of Fitness for a Particular Purpose

As the name demonstrates, this warranty includes the obligation that the product meets the needs of a particular purpose. For example, a certain shoe may be advertised as reliable for mountain climbing. However, if the shoe falls apart during the activity, this would constitute a breach of warranty of fitness for the particular purpose of mountain climbing.

Thus, although a product may be merchantable, it still may be a breach of the implied warranty of fitness for a particular purpose.

The Prima Facie Case

In pursuing a claim under breach of implied warranty of fitness, the burden of proof lies with the plaintiff to establish the following elements:

1. A communication from the buyer to the seller of the specific, intended purpose for which the product is being purchased;

2. The plaintiff's injury must arise while in use for that specific purpose;

3. The plaintiff must have relied on the defendant's expertise in selecting the particular product for its intended purpose;

Further, the defendant need not be a dealer in goods of that type in the regular course of his or her business.

INTENTIONAL TORTS

An intentional tort differs from an act of negligence in that—as the name implies—it requires the element of intent. In the context of product liability, the most common intentional tort would be fraudulent misrepresentation.

According to the Restatement of Torts 2nd, §402B, if a seller makes a material misrepresentation concerning the character or quality of goods, and the purchaser justifiably relies on that misrepresentation, the seller is liable for physical harm resulting from the failure of the product to conform to the representation.

Section 402B of the Restatement of Torts 2nd, with comments, is set forth at Appendix 1.

Misrepresentation sounds in tort, not contract, and is subject to strict liability even when the misrepresentation was innocently or negligently made, rather than fraudulent.

The Prima Facie Case

Some of the necessary elements to prove misrepresentation are:

1. The misrepresentation must be material; that is, it must be important enough to have influenced the purchaser's decision in selecting that particular product.

2. The purchaser must be aware of, and justifiably rely upon, the defendant's representation.

There are some advantages to bringing a claim for misrepresentation. If the plaintiff's jurisdiction does not permit punitive damages in contract claims, such damages may be available in a tortious misrepresentation action.

Further, this claim does not require a contractual relationship between the plaintiff and defendant, but extends to all foreseeable plaintiffs. Thus, a misrepresentation claim may be a viable alternative to a breach of warranty claim in jurisdictions which require privity of contract for the latter.

CHAPTER 5:
COMMON DEFENSES TO PRODUCT
LIABILITY CLAIMS

IN GENERAL

In response to a product liability claim, the defendant sets forth its defenses in its formal answer to the allegations contained in the plaintiff's complaint. Depending on the jurisdiction, some of those defenses are statutory, therefore, the reader is again cautioned to check the law of their own jurisdictions. Some of the most common defenses to product liability claims are set forth below.

STATUTE OF LIMITATIONS

The statute of limitations defense is common to all claims. In general, a statute of limitations refers to any law which sets forth a time period within which a claimant must bring a lawsuit to avoid being barred from enforcing a right or claim.

The time period varies according to the type of claim being made. The case must be filed before the expiration of the state's statute of limitations applicable to the particular action. The statute generally begins to run from the date of injury, or discovery of the injury.

The statute of limitations may be tolled—that is, suspended—under certain circumstances, such as the infancy of the plaintiff, or other statutory disability or tolling provision.

Some states have enacted statutes which are unique to product liability claims. For example, a statute of repose refers to the prohibition against product liability claims related to a product which has reached a certain age. The reasoning behind this statute is that the product is well worn by this time, and without any further useful life, it should no longer pose a risk to the manufacturer.

It is important that the reader check the law of their own jurisdictions concerning the applicable statute of limitations and tolling provisions.

INABILITY TO IDENTIFY THE PRODUCT

The plaintiff must be able to connect the product with the responsible party. Thus, the plaintiff must prove that the defendant either manufactured or sold the offending product. If the manufacturer can show that it never produced, distributed or sold the product in question, the claim will be dismissed.

Market Share Liability Exception

There is an exception in the area of drug litigation where the plaintiff cannot identify the particular pharmaceutical company who supplied the drug from among a number of manufacturers of the same drug. In this case, provided that the plaintiff can show which pharmaceutical companies marketed the particular drug, the doctrine of market share liability applies, and each manufacturer will be held liable according to its percentage of sales in the geographic area where the injury occurred.

ABSENCE OF PROXIMATE CAUSE

If the plaintiff cannot prove that the defect caused the injury, the defendant will prevail. Proximate causation must be rooted in fact—the cause-in-fact—and supported by a legal connection between the action and the injury.

For example, plaintiff is riding a bicycle on the road when, due to a defect in the construction of the bicycle, the wheel falls off. Plaintiff stops on the side of the road to repair the wheel. In the meantime, a car is speeding carelessly down the road and fails to see plaintiff on the side of the road. The driver of the car hits the plaintiff, who sustains serious injuries.

In this example, it is true that the bicycle defect was a cause-in-fact because had the plaintiff not stopped to repair the wheel, he would not have been struck by the car. However, the defect is not the proximate cause of the plaintiff's injuries. The negligence of the speeding driver is the superseding cause which led to plaintiff's injuries, and is thus the proximate cause.

DUTY, SUBSTANTIAL ALTERATION AND MISUSE

Duty refers to the obligation of the manufacturer or seller to use reasonable care to make sure that the product it produces or sells is safe for its ordinary use. This duty is not limited to the purchaser of the product, but extends to all foreseeable plaintiffs. If the defendant can show that it owed no duty to the plaintiff, or that it fulfilled its duty requirement, it will prevail.

The seller's duties are limited, and concern such responsibilities as inspecting the product for openly visible defects, and advising the purchaser of any known dangers associated with the use of the product. For this reason, the seller often prevails with the lack of duty defense.

It is the manufacturer's responsibility to make sure that there is no defect in the design or manufacture of the product, or in the warnings and instructions connected with the product, that will present an unreasonable danger.

Because the manufacturer has most of the responsibility in ensuring that the product is without defect, it is less likely to be able to prove lack of duty. When a manufacturer alleges lack of duty, it usually relates to some unforeseeable injury which was caused by the misuse of the product, or the substantial alteration of the product after its manufacture.

For example, the manufacturer of a chain saw uses reasonable care to make sure that the blade cannot come in contact with the user's hand during operation. It therefore installs a "state-of-the-art" shielding device on the unit which cannot be removed.

Nevertheless, the purchaser believes that he can work more efficiently if the shielding device was removed. Because the device is welded securely in place, the purchaser must use a blow torch to remove it. He is subsequently injured when he accidentally places his hand too close to the blade during operation. He sues the manufacturer.

The manufacturer will likely prevail because the purchaser made a substantial change to the product after it left the manufacturer's control, and it was this change that caused the purchaser's injury. Further, this misuse of the product was unforeseeable given the construction of the product.

A different result may occur if the shielding device was easily detachable, because any resulting injuries would arguably be foreseeable. This is known as "foreseeable misuse" for which the defendant would be held liable.

In addition, a manufacturer in a design defect case cannot claim as a defense that the product conformed with the industry standard. It could be that all such products, whether or not other manufacturers used the same design, are defective and the entire industry could be at fault for the particular design defect.

STATE-OF-THE-ART DEFENSE

Using the foregoing fact pattern, the defendant could also maintain that the chain saw with the unremovable shielding device was state-of-the-art and thus was not defective. State-of-the-art does not mean that a product merely conformed to an industry standard. A product is state-of-the-art when it is comparable to the safest of the functional alternative brands of similar products. Evidence of state-of-the-art shows that the defendant used reasonable care to make sure the product was designed in the safest possible manner.

Nevertheless, the state-of-the-art standard differs according to jurisdiction. Although some jurisdictions may permit industry custom to set the standard for state-of-the-art, other jurisdictions require a standard based on the existence of technology. The reader is cautioned to check the law of their jurisdictions on this point.

The state-of-the-art defense is applicable to negligence cases because such cases are conduct-oriented. A showing that the defendant used the safest possible design available will not result in a finding of fault in the conduct of the defendant.

However, because a strict liability claim is product-oriented, the state-of-the-art defense is irrelevant in those cases. Merely because a product is comparable to the safest of the functional alternative brands of similar products, if the product still presents a danger, its safety should be improved or it should not be marketed at all. A defendant should not be exonerated on that basis alone or it may deter—instead of encourage—product improvement.

THE UNAVOIDABLY UNSAFE PRODUCT DEFENSE

As set forth in Chapter 2, the unavoidably unsafe product is one which simply cannot be made safer given present knowledge or technology. Nevertheless, its usefulness outweighs its risks. This scenario is most often found in the area of drugs. Such products are excluded from those which are subject to strict liability.

PLAINTIFF'S CONTRIBUTORY FAULT

As further discussed in Chapter 6, the defendant may allege as a defense that the plaintiff's own actions contributed in some way to his or her injury. The reasonable person standard is used to determine whether the plaintiff's actions were prudent.

Depending on the jurisdiction, the plaintiff's assumption of risk, or contributory negligence—such as alteration or misuse of the product—may be a complete bar to recovery. Most jurisdictions, however, do not permit the contributory fault defense in the context of a strict liability claim.

As an alternative to the harshness of the recovery rules of contributory negligence and assumption of risk, some jurisdictions have enacted comparative negligence statutes, under which recovery may be diminished, but only according to the plaintiff's degree of culpability.

THE OBVIOUS DANGER AND SOPHISTICATED USER DEFENSES

The obvious danger and sophisticated user defenses both involve the user's knowledge, and what they should have known about the product.

Under the obvious danger rule, plaintiff's awareness of the danger is assumed if the danger is patently obvious. Although not a complete defense to liability, the obvious danger rule is a factor in the recovery analysis.

For example, if a danger is obvious, but the plaintiff ignores it, he or she will not likely be able to prevail under the theory that there was a failure by the manufacturer to warn about that danger.

Under the sophisticated user rule, the manufacturer or distributer generally would not be held liable if it failed to warn the user of a particular danger of which the user is aware, or is reasonably expected to be aware.

THE LEARNED INTERMEDIARY DEFENSE

As further set forth in Chapter 3, the learned intermediary defense refers to the defendant's duty to provide adequate warnings to a qualified person, who is then responsible for conveying those warnings to the user. This defense is most often used in the context of a physician/patient relationship.

For example, the manufacturer is required to give the physician correct and adequate warnings and instructions concerning a prescription drug. If it does so, it has fulfilled its duty and has shifted responsibility to the physician to provide his or her patient with the proper instructions and warnings on the use of the product.

A manufacturer may still be held liable if it does not provide adequate information to the physician. Further, in certain limited cases, the FDA requires that the patient be given this information directly. In such a case, a manufacturer may be held liable if he fails to comply with the FDA requirement.

DISCLAIMERS

A product may contain a disclaimer on its packaging which is used to deny or limit the remedies available to the injured plaintiff. There are certain requirements which must be met for a disclaimer to be considered valid:

1. The disclaimer must be conspicuously placed on the product. For example, a disclaimer which is located in small typeface on the inside cover of the product box would not likely be considered adequate.

2. The language of the disclaimer must be in terms clear enough for the average consumer to understand.

3. The disclaimer must not be unconscionable.

For example, a disclaimer cannot simply state that the manufacturer disclaims any liability if the product does not operate as advertised. This is fundamentally unfair to the consumer, who usually has no opportunity to test the product to determine whether it works, and relies on the representations made by the salesperson.

CHAPTER 6:
APPORTIONMENT OF LIABILITY

IN GENERAL

Once it has been established that there is indeed liability for the injuries sustained by the plaintiff, the extent of that liability, and its apportionment, must be determined. This chapter discusses the various forms liability takes, and how the plaintiff's own actions impact the liability of the defendants.

MARKET SHARE LIABILITY

Market share liability refers to the apportionment of liability among manufacturers when an individual defendant cannot be identified from a class of manufacturers of a specific product. Under this doctrine, each manufacturer is held liable according to its percentage of sales in the geographic area where the injury occurred.

This method of spreading the damages proportionally has been particularly useful in the context of drug litigation.

JOINT AND SEVERAL LIABILITY

Joint and several liability may be imposed when multiple parties are responsible for the plaintiff's injury. A distinction may be drawn between the actions of the defendants, as follows:

(1) Concerted Action—All defendants are responsible for the harm actually caused by only one.

(2) Independent Action—All defendants are responsible when defendants act independently, each causing harm to the plaintiff, but the degree cannot be allocated among them.

Case law has held that when two defendants are both negligent, but only one of them could have caused the plaintiff's injury, the court will hold both of them liable if it cannot determine which of the defendants caused the damage.

In such a case, it is the defendants who must come forward with evidence to absolve themselves. This shifts the burden of proof to the defendants. Otherwise, the plaintiff would never be able to prove who actually caused the injury.

CONTRIBUTORY FAULT

Contributory fault refers to those situations in which the plaintiff's own actions contribute in some way to his or her harm.

Assumption of Risk

Assumption of risk refers to the common-law doctrine which states that a plaintiff may not recover for an injury when he has voluntarily exposed himself to a known danger.

Contributory Negligence

Contributory negligence refers to conduct on the part of the plaintiff which falls below the standard to which he or she should conform for his or her own protection, and which is a legally contributing cause cooperating with the negligence of the defendant in bringing the plaintiff harm.

The burden of proving the plaintiff's contributory negligence is on the defense. If contributory negligence is found, under the common law, the plaintiff was barred from recovery. There are exceptions, as set forth below.

Comparative Negligence

Comparative negligence refers to a statute change introduced in many jurisdictions to counteract the harshness of the recovery rules of contributory negligence and assumption of risk. Under comparative negligence rules, recovery may be diminished, but only according to the plaintiff's degree of culpability.

VICARIOUS LIABILITY

When third persons are held liable for the conduct of others, they are said to be vicariously liable. We assume both the identity of the actor and the wrongful nature of his or her conduct, and ask whether liability may be extended beyond the actor to include persons who have not committed a wrong or directly caused any harm, but on whose behalf the wrongdoing actor acted.

The concept of vicarious liability is one of considerable practical importance to the plaintiff because it is an effective means of providing a financially responsible defendant. For example, in certain situations, employers may be held liable for the torts of their employees. This principle is derived from the common law master/servant relationship and is known as the doctrine of "respondeat superior." This doctrine, as well as other forms of vicarious liability relationships, are explained below.

Respondeat Superior

The most important principle establishing vicarious liability for the tortious conduct of another is the doctrine of respondeat superior: A master is vicariously liable for the torts of his servants committed while the latter are acting within the scope of their employment.

For example, in the context of a breach of warranty claim, a sales clerk for a shoe store may represent to the plaintiff that certain hiking boots are suitable for rock climbing, which is the plaintiff's stated purpose for the purchase. If that representation turns out to be false, and the plaintiff is injured during the activity of rock climbing due to failure of the boots, the store owner would likely be responsible for the breach under the respondeat superior doctrine.

The "servant" need not be performing precisely the activity for which he was hired in order to expose the master to liability, and the tortious conduct need not involve physical injury. Thus, the officers of our major corporations are considered "servants" in the legal sense of the word. Also, the "servant" need not be receiving a wage, but may be performing services out of a sense of friendship for another.

In contrast to "servants," independent contractors are persons hired to do jobs under circumstances which, as a general rule, do not call for the application of the doctrine of respondeat superior.

If the tortfeasor is an independent contractor, the general rule is that the employer is not vicariously liable for the harm caused by the contractor's wrongful conduct.

Joint Enterprise

When two or more persons join together in an enterprise in which each has an equal right to control the other's conduct, one might apply master-servant concepts upon each participant in relation to the other participant. For example, in a partnership, each partner is generally liable for the acts of the other partners.

Successor Corporation Liability

When Corporation A and Corporation B conduct a formal merger and become Corporation C, C is liable for the torts that A and B may have committed prior to the merger.

DEATH OF AN INJURED PARTY PRIOR TO JUDGMENT

One may be under the impression that if the injured party dies before there is a recovery, the defendant is "off the hook." However, by statute, the death of the injured party prior to judgment has far less devastating effects upon existing or potential rights to recover against a tortious defendant. The following two types of statutes accomplish this result:

Survival Statutes

Survival statutes prevent abatement of existing causes of action due to the death of either party. The basic measure of recovery is what the decedent would have been able to recover for the injuries if he or she had survived.

Wrongful Death Statutes

Wrongful death statutes create causes of action that allow recovery when the tortious conduct of the defendant causes someone to die. The basic measure of recovery is the harm caused to the decedent's family by the defendant's conduct.

A table setting forth the state wrongful death statutes is set forth in the Appendix 5.

CHAPTER 7:
DAMAGES AND CLAIM RESOLUTION

IN GENERAL

Once it has been determined that there is liability, the question turns to whether damages were caused as a result of the wrongful conduct. In personal injury law, damages are usually measured in terms of monetary compensation. There are three categories of money damages recoverable in a personal injury case: (1) compensatory damages; (2) punitive damages, and (3) nominal damages.

COMPENSATORY DAMAGES

Compensatory damages represent an attempt to compensate the injured party for the actual harm he suffered, by awarding the amount of money necessary to restore the plaintiff to his pre-injury condition. Often, a complete restoration cannot be accomplished.

In such cases, damages also include the monetary value of the difference between the plaintiff's pre-injury and post-injury conditions. Typical items include those listed below.

Medical Expenses

Medical expenses are the most concrete and objectively demonstrable items to identify. The expense must be reasonably related to the defendant's wrongful conduct.

Lost Earnings and Impairment of Earning Capacity

Lost earnings and impairment of earning capacity are the most justifiable element of a general compensatory damages award from a strictly economic point of view. Recovery is sought for:

(1) the earnings actually lost up to the time of the trial or settlement; and

(2) the diminution in the plaintiff's capacity to earn in the future.

Pain, Suffering, and Other Intangible Elements

Pain and suffering is the most difficult element of recovery to measure. This is a broad concept, which may include a number of more or less separate factors, the most common of which is the physical pain associated with the injury. Recovery for mental suffering associated with bodily disfigurement may also be included as an element of pain and suffering.

Another element is the loss of enjoyment in relation to life in either all of its aspects, or merely certain aspects. This is also known as hedonic damages.

For example, if a plaintiff enjoyed playing piano as a hobby, and has suffered an injury to his hands, the plaintiff has suffered a loss of enjoyment in relation to the ability to play the piano.

Of course, if the particular activity involved the plaintiff's livelihood, the damages for loss of earning capacity would also be included, and would greatly increase the measure of damages.

Injury to Personal Property

The rules in case of injury to personal property are simple and straightforward. The basic measure is the difference between the market value of the property before the injury and its market value after.

If the property has been totally destroyed, the market value after the injury will be the salvage value, if any. The cost of repairs are included, in addition to payment for devaluation, if any, after repair. The plaintiff may also be able to recover for the loss of use of the property while it is repaired or replaced, as long as it is within a reasonable time period.

PUNITIVE DAMAGES

Punitive damages involve an award of a substantial amount of money to the plaintiff for the purpose of punishing the defendant. Thus, punitive damages are usually only awarded if the defendant acted intentionally, or with reckless indifference to the plaintiff.

Liability insurance is the usual source of recovery for personal injury claims. However, in cases involving intentional torts, insurance generally does not cover the wrongdoer. In the absence of insurance coverage, claims must be paid out of the defendant's personal assets.

NOMINAL DAMAGES

A nominal damages award involves a very small amount of money, awarded merely for the purpose of showing that the plaintiff was legally wronged, particularly where the injuries sustained, if any, are inconsequential.

CLAIM RESOLUTION

As set forth below, a personal injury claim may be resolved by (a) going through a trial and obtaining a verdict; (b) alternative dispute resolution; and (c) negotiation and settlement.

Litigation and Verdict

Litigation is the most formal, and the most time-consuming of the dispute resolution methods. Litigation is complicated, costly, and can go on for years. The parties to the litigation are each responsible for developing their own legal theory, and providing their evidence, in order to prove their case and prevail in the dispute. The judge or jury considers all of the evidence and arguments set forth by the parties. Once the parties have set forth their case, the judge or jury is entrusted to make the final decision.

The final resolution of litigation occurs when the finder of fact—the judge or jury—renders a verdict for either the plaintiff or the defense. In a bifurcated trial, the issue of liability is resolved first and, if liability is determined, a second trial is held to determine the extent of the damages suffered by the plaintiff, and the apportionment of the liability. If there is a defense verdict, the case is dismissed and the plaintiff loses. Of course, the plaintiff always has the option of appealing the decision if there are adequate grounds to support an appeal.

Alternative Dispute Resolution

Alternative dispute resolution (ADR) refers to the practice of resolving a disagreement to the satisfaction of all parties, in an expedient and economically feasible manner, rather than litigating the dispute. Another advantage of alternative dispute resolution is that it affords the parties complete confidentiality, unlike court records which are open to the public.

There are various methods of alternative dispute resolution, with differing degrees of formality. The primary methods of alternative dispute resolution include (i) arbitration and (ii) mediation.

Arbitration

Arbitration is the process whereby an impartial third party, known as an arbitrator, listens to both sides of the dispute and issues a binding decision.

Mediation

Mediation is a less formal method of alternative dispute resolution than arbitration. Mediation, like arbitration, enlists the assistance of a neutral third party, known as a mediator. However, the role of the mediator differs from that of the arbitrator. The mediator does not issue a binding decision but rather assists the opposing parties in resolving their own dispute, which resolution may then be formalized in a written agreement.

For a more detailed discussion of alternative dispute resolution, the reader is advised to consult this author's legal almanac entitled The Law of Alternative Dispute Resolution, also published by Oceana Publishing Company.

Negotiation and Settlement

Negotiation is the least formal method of resolving a dispute without litigation. For negotiation to succeed, the participants must be able to openly and patiently communicate with each other, even though they may disagree. Negotiation follows no established rules or guidelines. It is entirely voluntary and conducted between the parties to the negotiation, or their representatives. There are no third party intermediaries available to assist the negotiators in reaching a settlement.

Negotiation presents a scenario of offers and counter-offers concerning resolution of a particular dispute, until the parties reach that magic middle ground on which they can mutually agree—the settlement. A settlement is a mutual agreement to terminate the dispute for consideration—usually the payment of a sum of money.

A settlement may be judicial or non-judicial. A non-judicial settlement is one which is reached between the parties without court intervention. A judicial settlement is one which is reached during the pendency of a lawsuit, usually with the supervision and guidance of the trial judge. In general, the policy of all courts is to encourage settlement and discourage litigation.

If the party being sued is insured for that type of claim, the insurance company has an obligation to settle a case in good faith. If the company is presented with a settlement opportunity that is within the policy limit, it should settle the case unless there is strong evidence that the case has no merit. If the insurance company refuses to settle a meritorious claim, it could be held liable for payment of any excess above the policy limit which may be awarded after trial.

Once an agreement has been reached, a final written document encompassing all of the negotiated points should be drafted and signed by the parties. Depending on the nature of the dispute, a settlement agreement may also include a release of claims. By signing a release, a party gives up all right to pursue the claims stated in the release. This is both the motivation and consideration for entering into the settlement agreement.

A sample settlement agreement and release of claims in a product liability case is set forth at Appendix 6.

Types of Settlements

The primary types of settlement agreements include:

Lump Sum Settlement

The lump sum settlement is the most common type of settlement, which generally requires the payment of a sum of money in exchange for the release of the other party's claims.

Sliding-Scale Settlement

A sliding scale settlement includes a condition in which it is agreed that an adjustment may be made to the settling defendant's obligation dependent upon any amounts which may ultimately be recovered from the nonsettling defendants.

Structured Settlement

The structure settlement allows for the payment of money, in installments, over a period of time. The structured settlement is usually used when the recovery is significant and the paying party is financially unable to make a lump sum payment, or in cases involving minors. Generally, the plaintiff receives payments from a trust or annuity which is funded by the defendant.

Disbursement of Funds

Once the necessary paperwork has been completed—i.e., the order, arbitration award or settlement agreement—a check or draft is drawn up by the defendant, or its insurance company, and is generally made payable to both the plaintiff client and his or her attorney.

The attorney usually deposits the check in an attorney trust account for disbursement of funds. The costs of litigation are generally deducted from the gross recovery. The attorney then calculates his or her legal fee according to the terms of the retainer agreement.

A sample retainer agreement in a product liability action is set forth at Appendix 7.

ADVANTAGES OF SUCCESSFUL PRODUCT LIABILITY LITIGATION

As a result of successful product liability litigation, manufacturers are producing safer products. Manufacturers know that if they manufacture a product that is unreasonably dangerous, they subject themselves to liability and the possibility of a large verdict. Therefore, for example, they take greater efforts in keeping unsafe products out of the marketplace and issuing product safety recalls for products found to be dangerous once they have reached the consumer.

A sample product safety recall notice by the U.S. Consumer Product Safety Commission is set forth at Appendix 8.

Thus, through the means of a product liability lawsuit, the consumer has the power to ensure that the products entering the marketplace are safe.

In order to document an injury caused by an unsafe product, consumers can file a Consumer Product Incident Report with the U.S. Consumer Product Safety Commission and the claim will be investigated.

A sample Consumer Product Incident Report is set forth at Appendix 9.

CHAPTER 8:
TOBACCO PRODUCTS LIABILITY

IN GENERAL

Cigarette smoking is the single most preventable cause of premature death in the United States. According to the Centers for Disease Control (CDC), an estimated 47 million adults in the United States smoke cigarettes even though this single behavior will result in death or disability for half of all regular users. Cigarette smoking is responsible for more than 430,000 deaths each year, or one in every five deaths. In addition, the medical costs associated with smoking-related illness is staggering, totalling between $50 billion and $73 billion in medical expenditures and another $50 billion in indirect costs.

Since the release in 1964 of the first Surgeon General's report on smoking and health, the scientific knowledge about the health consequences of tobacco use has greatly increased. It is now well documented that smoking can cause chronic lung disease, coronary heart disease, and stroke, as well as cancer of the lungs, larynx, esophagus, mouth, and bladder. In addition, smoking contributes to cancer of the cervix, pancreas, and kidneys. Researchers have identified more than 40 chemicals in tobacco smoke that cause cancer in humans and animals.

In addition, women who use tobacco during pregnancy are more likely to have adverse birth outcomes, including babies with low birth weight, which is linked with an increased risk of infant death and with a variety of infant health disorders.

A table setting forth tobacco use in the United States demographically for adults aged 18 and older is set forth at Appendix 10.

YOUTH AND TOBACCO

The tobacco industry has been criticized for targeting children and young adults in their advertising campaign. Despite their denial, the fact is that advertising has been successful in bringing in new customers from this young and impressionable age group.

According to a 1997 report, 5,318,682 of our nation's youth are projected to die prematurely from their smoking. According to the Centers for Disease Control, more than a quarter (28.4 percent) of high school students were current cigarette smokers, with male and female students smoking at equal rates—28.7 and 28.2 percent respectively.

Children as young as middle school age are also smoking. According to the Centers for Disease Control, current cigarette use among middle school students was 9.2 percent—9.6 percent of whom were males and 8.8 percent were females.

PREVENTIVE MEASURES—THE CENTERS FOR DISEASE CONTROL (CDC)

A number of preventive measures have been undertaken in order to decrease cigarette smoking. These include (a) school-based health education; (b) reducing minors' access to tobacco products; (c) more extensive counseling by health-care providers about smoking cessation; (d) developing and enacting strong, clean indoor air policies and laws; (e) restricting or eliminating advertising targeted toward persons aged less than 18 years; and (f) increasing tobacco excise taxes.

With fiscal year 2001 funds, the Centers for Disease Control provide support for preventing and controlling tobacco use in all 50 states, 7 territories, 6 tribal-serving organizations, and the District of Columbia. The CDC also offers technical assistance to states on planning, developing, implementing, and evaluating tobacco control programs.

To help prevent tobacco use at its most crucial point—during adolescence—the CDC provided grants to 21 states in fiscal year 2000 for coordinated school health programs that include components for preventing tobacco use.

The CDC also develops and distributes tobacco and health information natonwide. For example, the CDC responds to more than 93,000 tobacco-related requests annually, of which 40,000 are made through the Internet. In the past year, the CDC distributed more than 1.5 million publications and video products. In addition, the CDC provides ready access to tobacco use prevention information and databases through its website at http://www.cdc.gov/.

In addition to federal resources, support for a nationwide system of tobacco control is available in some states through monies from increased tobacco excise taxes, legal settlements with the tobacco industry, and grants awarded by the American Legacy Foundation.

THE TOBACCO PRODUCTS LIABILITY PROJECT

The Tobacco Products Liability Project (TPLP) was founded in 1984 by doctors, academics and attorneys for the purpose of coordinating both products liability suits against the tobacco industry and lobbying for legislative and regulatory initiatives to control the sale and use of tobacco.

The TPLP's activities include sponsoring an annual conference, workshops and lectures; hosting an attorney referral service; providing an information clearinghouse; filing amicus curiae briefs in tobacco lawsuits; testifying before Congress; and performing legal research and analysis to support states and municipalities pass tobacco control measures.

Tobacco Products Liability Lawsuits

Tobacco products liability lawsuits are designed to increase public awareness about the dangers of cigarette smoking and decrease the profit intake of the tobacco industry by causing them to incur legal costs. In turn, this decrease in profit results in a price increase which discourages tobacco use. In general, the plaintiff brings a lawsuit alleging that nicotine addition has caused their particular injury, e.g. lung cancer. The tobacco industry commonly defends such a claim by stating that the plaintiff ignored all of the available information on the health risks of smoking and willingly continued the activity.

Tobacco products liability lawsuits were brought by the Attorneys General of 44 states against the tobacco industry. Four of the states suing the tobacco industry reached settlements with the tobacco defendants. The remaining states signed a Master Settlement Agreement in November of 1998.

The text of the tobacco products liability complaint in the Commonwealth of Massachussetts, et. al, Plaintiffs, vs. Philip Morris, Inc., et. al., Defendants, is set forth at Appendix 11.

Tobacco Control Measures

The TPLP assists states and municipalities in passing tobacco control measures by providing legal assistance. The TPLP ensures that such measures are enacted in a legally valid manner and drafted so as to be able to withstand legal challenges by the tobacco industry.

A chart and explanation of some of the most recent tobacco control measures enacted is set forth at Appendix 12.

SECOND-HAND SMOKE

The health of nonsmokers is adversely affected by environmental tobacco smoke (ETS)—also referred to as "second hand smoke." Each year, exposure to second hand smoke causes an estimated 3,000 nonsmoking Americans to die of lung cancer and causes up to 300,000 children to suffer from lower respiratory tract infections. Evidence also indicates that exposure to second hand smoke increases the risk of coronary heart disease.

Las Vegas casino dealers, who are often exposed to years of second-hand cigarette smoke, have initiated a lawsuit seeking the creation of a medical monitoring program paid for by tobacco companies to detect the possible onset of lung cancer or heart disease and treat the development of smoking-related illnesses. The plaintiffs argue that the dealers were not made aware of the health risks of second hand smoke and the tobacco companies knew that second hand smoke was harmful.

The proposed class consists of as many as 45,000 casino employees who have been exposed to second-hand smoke but who have not yet developed medical problems related to the exposure. The suit names 17 tobacco companies and organizations.

Attorneys for the tobacco companies are defending the action and requesting the court to reject the request for medical monitoring. They argued that granting such a request is dangerous in that it would open a new and costly legal claim based not on a medical problem but on the increased risk of a medical problem.

CHAPTER 9:
PRODUCT LIABILITY IN THE MEDICAL SETTING

MEDICATIONS

Pharmaceutical companies owe a duty to the consumer to ensure that the medications they manufacture and sell are reasonably safe when used by the consumer as intended. To make sure that the drug is safe, the manufacturer must properly research the drug's possible side effects and risks before putting it on the market. Although a particular drug may have been given FDA approval, this does not guarantee that the product is safe. The pharmaceutical manufacturer must also make sure that the medication is accompanied by thorough warnings which ensure that the public is adequately informed of any risks associated with the medication.

Non-Prescription Drugs

Medications which are sold over the counter must be accompanied by an adequate warning to inform the public of the nature of the drug, and any side effects and risks. The manufacturer must convey this warning to the public by using proper labeling on the package and informative package inserts. This is especially important when the manufacturer knows of risks connected with ingestion of the non-prescription drug and this information is not likely to be known by the consumer. In the case of non-prescription drugs, the pharmaceutical manufacturer owes a direct duty to the consumer.

It is a fact that certain drugs, which may pose no threat when taken alone, can not be used in conjunction with other drugs. Thus, while a patient may be on one over-the-counter drug, prescription of another drug may cause harmful effects, and even death, when the two drugs are used together. This is especially true with certain drugs like anti-depressants and also drugs for high blood pressure. The consumer is advised to check with both the physician and pharmacist when taking any combination of drugs, whether they are prescription or non-prescription.

Prescription Drugs

In the case of prescription drugs, the pharmaceutical manufacturer's duty is to the physician, as a "learned intermediary," instead of to the consumer directly. Thus, the manufacturer's liability is limited provided it properly and adequately informs the physicians of all of the risks associated with the particular drug.

For example, a particular prescription drug may be suitable for adults but not deemed suitable for children. If the pharmaceutical manufacturer fails to adequately warn physicians that the particular medication should not be prescribed for children, an otherwise safe drug becomes unreasonably dangerous due to the manufacturer's failure to warn.

Physician's Duty—The Learned Intermediary

Physicians, as learned intermediaries, have a duty to advise the patient of all of the risks and side effects of medications the physician prescribes. This ensures that the patient is able to make an informed decision about whether they will take the medication. If the physician fails to advise the patient of the manufacturer's warning, or otherwise neglects the warnings provided by the manufacturer, the physician is negligent and will be liable for any resulting injuries to the patient.

Using the foregoing example, if the manufacturer adequately informed the physician that the particular drug was not suitable for children, and the physician ignored this warning and prescribed the medication for a child, the physician will be liable to the patient for any injuries which may occur as a result of the drug.

The physician's duty stems from his or her superior medical knowledge. It is presumed that the physician knows that the patient relies on the physician's knowledge and judgment. As a learned intermediary, it is also presumed that the physician, who has been given adequate information concerning a particular medication, is in the best position to know whether that medication should be prescribed for a particular patient.

If a physician is not familiar with particular medication, prior to prescribing the drug, they will generally consult the Physicians' Desk Reference (PDR) for detailed information about the drug, its side effects, and interactions with other drugs. In the PDR, the doctor can learn everything necessary for the safe use of a drug.

Pharmaceutical Liability Lawsuit

If a patient suffers injuries as a result of a particular medication, he or she can bring a lawsuit against the drug manufacturer under all of the usual product liability theories—e.g., strict liability, negligence, and breach of warranty. However, if it is the physician's conduct which is at fault for not heeding the warnings and information provided by the manufacturer, then the physician may be sued for medical negligence in a medical malpractice lawsuit.

An example of pharmaceutical liability involves the drug Fenfluramine, commonly referred to as "Fen-Phen." Fen-Phen was the subject of litigation initiated against the manufacturers of the drug. This drug was manufactured and sold by many different generic names for the purpose of weight loss. It is claimed that the drug caused medical problems such as primary pulmonary hypertension, valvular heart disease, and neurotoxicity.

In 1997, the FDA issued a "FDA Public Health Advisory" to all health care professionals bringing to their attention the recent reports of valvular heart disease and primary pulmonary hypertension associated with fen-phen. Shortly thereafter, the drug was taken off the market. The plaintiffs claim that the pharmaceutical company withheld information from the patients, pharmacies and doctors about the reports it had received of illnesses and injuries and their association with this drug. Internal corporate memos were produced which demonstrated that the manufacturer was aware of this connection.

It is important, when considering any lawsuit based on pharmaceutical liability, that you obtain a print-out of your pharmacy records from the pharmacy or pharmacies where you purchased the drug.

MEDICAL DEVICES

Manufacturers of medical devices are liable for any defects in the devices which cause injury to the consumer. Unlike other products, medical devices for use and sale in the United States are governed by the Food and Drug Administration (FDA) under the 1976 Medical Device Amendments to the Food, Drug & Cosmetic Act. This Act sought to provide "reasonable assurance of safety and effectiveness" for all medical devices.

Classes of Medical Devices

The FDA has grouped medical devices into three classes—designated as Class I, Class II and Class III—based upon the amount of risk involved in the use of the device. Each device is also divided into seven different categories which relate to the 1976 amendment: (i) pre-market; (ii) post-market; (iii) substantially equivalent; (iv) implant; (v) custom; (vi) investigational; and (vii) transitional. The classes and categories devised by the FDA determine the level of scrutiny that a device must undergo in order to reach the marketplace.

Class III medical devices consist of those devices which are deemed to present a potentially unreasonable risk of injury. Medical devices which are deemed to fall into the "substantially equivalent" category have been the source of much of the medical device-related litigation.

Devices are "substantially equivalent" if the FDA finds that a device which was in existence and use prior to the 1976 amendment is substantially equivalent to a device which is presently proposed to be marketed. The medical device is deemed to have been "tested by time" and thus rigorous testing of the device is generally not required.

However, medical device liability lawsuits often arise when the manufacturer proposes to have a particular device improperly placed in the "substantially equivalent" category. The manufacturer fails to report that the particular device in fact has substantial differences to the pre-existing device. The manufacturer is obviously concerned with cutting costs by trying to sidestep the testing process and gain immediate approval to place the device on the market.

Physician's Duty

As with prescription medications, a doctor is also obligated to disclose to his or her patients all of the risks associated with using a particular medical device being prescribed for the patient. Failure to provide such informed consent may give rise to a claim for medical negligence against the doctor.

CHAPTER 10:
TOXIC TORTS

IN GENERAL

A toxic tort is a tort caused by an individual's contact with a toxic substance. After the Industrial Revolution, a number of dangerous, toxic substances have been introduced to the environment. Some of the worst offending toxic substances responsible for injuries include the following:

1. Lead-based paint—Associated withi brain damage, especially in children;

2. Asbestos—Associated with lung cancer and lung disease, such as mesothelioma;

3. Dry cleaning Solvents—Associated witih brain damage and major organ damage;

4. Pesticides—Associated with birth injuries;

5. Electro-magnetic fields from utility wires or major appliances—Associated with cancer.

6. Toxic landfill waste—Associated with leukemia and other syndromes.

Corporate America has been critcized and accused of greed for failing to protect the public from dangers associated with such toxic material. However, the lack of adequate governmental regulation in the use and disposal of toxic substances has made it easier for the corporations to ignore the problem.

ASBESTOS EXPOSURE

A common toxic tort lawsuit involves exposure to asbestos. Asbestos is a naturally occurring silicate mineral that can be separated into fibers. The fibers are long, thin, flexible, strong, durable, and resistant to heat and fire. Asbestos has been used in thousands of consumer, industrial, maritime, automotive, scientific and building products. During the twentieth century, some 30 million tons of asbestos were used in industrial sites, homes, schools, shipyards and commercial buildings in the United States.

As a result of exposure to asbestos, many individuals have developed asbestos-related diseases, including mesothelioma. Mesothelioma is a cancer of the cells that make up the lining around the outside of the lungs and inside of the ribs or around the abdominal organs. The only known cause of mesothelioma in the United States is previous exposure to asbestos fibers.

Liability stems from the fact that asbestos manufacturers knew about the hazards of asbestos seventy years ago, but they kept this knowledge to themselves and for many years failed to warn workers and others who might be exposed to asbestos fibers. The first warnings to workers exposed to asbestos were not given until the mid-1960s but the warnings given were wholly inadequate. It is a fact that workers are still not adequately warned that they are working around asbestos and are at risk for asbestos disease.

In 1995, OSHA issued workplace standards for testing, maintenance and disclosure of asbestos. Rental property owners were also covered by thes OSHA regulations. Unless the property owner rules out the presence of asbestos through testing, it is presumed that asbestos is present.

When a landlord complies with OSHA regulations, performs testing, and discovers friable asbestos in a rental property, the landlord is obligated to disclose this hidden and dangerous defect to the tenants. The presence of friable asbestos in rental property might be considered a breach of the implied warranty of habitability, and a tenant may be able to seek legal remedies.

Asbestos-containing products were also used extensively in the construction of schools and other public buildings until the 1970's. In 1986, Congress passed the Asbestos Hazard Emergency Response Act (AHERA) to protect public and private school children and school employees from asbestos exposure.

Under the terms of the Act, each school must designate and train a person to oversee asbestos-related activities in the school; all buildings must be inspected for the presence of asbestos-containing materials; a management plan for controlling asbestos exposure must be developed, using accredited inspection personnel to implement the plan; all records should be available for public review; and all teachers, parents and employees should be informed annually about the asbestos-related activities in the school. In the past school districts have been fined for failing to meet provisions of AHERA.

CAUSATION AND BURDEN OF PROOF

It is generally a difficult task for an attorney to prove that an individual has been injured by a particular toxic substance, particularly given the fact that the injuries associated with exposure may not manifest themselves for many years following exposure. Meeting the burden of proof requires that the attorney have a complete understanding of the particular toxin. It is often necessary to consult with a number of experts who are experienced with diagnosing and treating toxic exposure.

A plaintiff complaining of toxic exposure is not obligated to prove his or her case "beyond a reasonable doubt" as is required of a prosecutor in a criminal case. The toxic tort plaintiff must merely prove that his or her claims are more likely true than not—a much lesser burden of proof to sustain.

DEFENSES

The responsible parties in toxic exposure cases, including the manufacturers and users of toxic substances, defend these cases vigorously. There have been cases where the particular corporation has even resorted to doctoring and/or destroying documentary evidence which would support the plaintiff's claim, such as in-house reports which demonstrate that the corporation had knowledge of the potential harm associated with a particular toxic substance.

Other common defenses include allegations that the individual is not injured, or that the individual's injuries were caused by something other than the toxic substance, and often attack the credibility of the plaintiff.

CLASS ACTION LAWSUITS

Oftentimes when there has been some type of toxic exposure, it affects a group of people rather than an individual. This is especially so in cases of environmental contamination. In order to most expeditiously bring a lawsuit representing all of the injured persons, the law allows those affected to bring the lawsuit as a group rather than bringing a number of individual lawsuits. This is known as a class action. This helps to level the playing field with wealthy corporations as there is strength in numbers. In addition, the class action is crucial in promoting judicial economy.

DAMAGES

A toxic tort plaintiff who prevails in a lawsuit and proves that his or her injuries were caused by exposure to the toxic substance, and that the manufacturer of the toxic substance was negligent or careless, is entitled to collect money damages. Compensation may be awarded for the following:

1. The cost of past and future medical care;

2. The cost of necessary rehabilitation;

3. The loss of past and future wages;

4. The loss of earning capacity;

5. The loss of enjoyment of life; and

6. The pain and suffering associated with the toxic exposure.

PREVENTION

In order to minimize exposure to toxic substances, people are advised not to move into areas where there are large electrical towers and transformers, chemical plants, oil refineries, manufacturing plants, rail yards, landfills and any bodies of water located downstream from such facilities.

One should also make sure that their intended home is free of asbestos and lead-based paint, particularly if they have small children. Prior to purchasing a home, a building inspector can take certain tests to determine whether any such toxic substances are present in the home.

If there has been a potential exposure to a toxic substance, contact your family physician for immediate treatment. Depending on the nature and location of the exposure, reports should also be made to the United States Environmental Protection Agency; the United States Occupational Health and Safety Administration; the state Department of Environmental Resources; and the state or local Department of Health.

LEAD-BASED PAINT POISONING

As set forth above, one of the most common toxic substances to which people—particularly young children—have been exposed is lead-based paint. Because of the hazards associated with lead-based paint, the use of lead in paint was banned in America in 1978. The greatest risk of injury from lead poisoning is to children under the age of seven. The young child's brain and body is sensitive to lead, even in small amounts. Exposure can cause irreversible injury to the child, which may not be evident until many years following exposure. The following injuries have been found to be associated with lead-based paint poisoning:

1. Learning disabilities;

2. Brain damage;

3. Loss of IQ points and intellect;

4. Academic failure;

5. Neuropsychological deficits;

6. Attention deficit disorder;

7. Hyperactive behavior;

8. Antisocial behavior;

9. Neurological problems;

10. Swelling of the brain;

11. Major organ failure;

12. Coma; and

13. Death.

Thus, lead-poisoning can rob a child of his or her future, severely diminishing his or her mental and physical capacity and ability to be self-sufficient, and even causing their death.

Level of Exposure

According to the The United States Centers for Disease Control and Prevention in Atlanta (CDC), the risk of injury begins when the level of lead in a child's blood rises to 10 micrograms per deciliter of whole blood. Once the lead is ingested, it causes permanent damage to the child. The only recourse is to prevent further exposure and provide medical intervention to help the child excrete any lead that has been ingested.

Source of Exposure

The most common source of lead-based paint poisoning in a child is deteriorating lead-based paint located on the exterior and interior of the child's home. The deteriorated lead-based paint becomes lead paint chips, which the child may eat, and lead-contaminated paint dust, which children ingest.

Prevention

When buying or renting a home, one should err on the side of precaution, particularly if they have children under the age of seven, and assume that there is lead in the paint of a house that was built prior to 1978—the year the law banning lead in paint was passed. The prospective buyer or tenant should request a lead-based paint inspection and, if lead is found in the paint, they should request that the seller or landlord remove any deteriorating paint and repaint with non-leaded paint. If you are already residing in the home where lead-based paint is found, it is important to keep the floors and walls clean and make sure that young children wash their hands and avoid putting their toys and other objects in their mouth until the problem has been addressed.

If a child exhibits the symptoms listed below, they should receive immediate medical care:

(a) Sluggish behavior;

(b) Apathy;

(c) Headaches;

(d) Periods of staring;

(e) Tremors;

(f) Seizures ;

(g) Loss of consciousness;

(h) Abdominal cramps;

(i) Loss of appetite;

(j) Constipation;

(k) Irritability;

(l) Hyperactive behaviors.

Parents can obtain more detailed information from the National Lead Information Center (1-800-LEAD-FYI).

Lead-Based Paint Lawsuits

Lawsuits are brought against negligent landlords on behalf of children who have suffered injuries due to lead-based paint poisoning. Such lawsuits may arise as a result of a landlord's refusal to obey local and federal health and housing codes and regulations, or refusal to comply with a tenant's request for repainting, or the landlord's neglect of deteriorating paint on the premises.

As with any toxic tort case, plaintiffs who have been injured as a result of lead-paint poisoning, and prevail in their lawsuit, are entitled to be compensated by those who are responsible. This is particularly important for children who have suffered mild to moderate brain damage as a result of the exposure.

As is the case with most toxic tort lawsuits, lead-based paint lawsuits are vigorously defended by landlords. Their defense usually focuses on the theory that any deficits that the child exhibits are due to factors other than ingestion of lead-based paint.

APPENDIX 1:
THE PRODUCT LIABILITY FAIRNESS ACT

SEECTION 1. SHORT TITLE.

This Act may be cited as the 'Product Liability Fairness Act of 1995'.

TITLE I—PRODUCT LIABILITY

SEC. 101. DEFINITIONS. For purposes of this Act, the following definitions shall apply:

(1) Actual malice: The term 'actual malice' means specific intent to cause serious physical injury, illness, disease, or damage to property, or death.

(2) Claimant: The term 'claimant' means any person who brings a product liability action and any person on whose behalf such an action is brought. If an action is brought through or on behalf of—

(A) an estate, the term includes the decedent; or

(B) a minor or incompetent, the term includes the legal guardian of the minor or incompetent.

(3) Claimant's benefits: The term 'claimant's benefits' means the amount paid to an employee as workers' compensation benefits.

(4) Clear and convincing evidence:

(A) In general: Subject to subparagraph (A), the term 'clear and convincing evidence' is that measure of degree of proof that will produce in the mind of the trier of fact a firm belief or conviction as to the truth of the allegations sought to be established.

(B) Degree of proof: The degree of proof required to satisfy the standard of clear and convincing evidence shall be—

(i) greater than the degree of proof required to meet the standard of preponderance of the evidence; and

(ii) less than the degree of proof required to meet the standard of proof beyond a reasonable doubt.

(5) Commercial loss: The term 'commercial loss' means any loss or damage to a product itself, loss relating to a dispute over its value, or consequential economic loss the recovery of which is governed by the Uniform Commercial Code or analogous State commercial law, not including harm.

(6) Durable good: The term 'durable good' means any product, or any component of any such product, which has a normal life expectancy of 3 or more years or is of a character subject to allowance for depreciation under the Internal Revenue Code of 1986, and which is—

(A) used in a trade or business;

(B) held for the production of income; or

(C) sold or donated to a governmental or private entity for the production of goods, training, demonstration, or any other similar purpose.

(7) Economic loss: The term 'economic loss' means any pecuniary loss resulting from harm (including any medical expense loss, work loss, replacement services loss, loss due to death, burial costs, and loss of business or employment opportunities), to the extent that recovery for the loss is permitted under applicable State law.

(8) Harm: The term 'harm' means any physical injury, illness, disease, or death, or damage to property, caused by a product. The term does not include commercial loss or loss or damage to a product itself.

(9) Insurer: The term 'insurer' means the employer of a claimant, if the employer is self-insured, or the workers' compensation insurer of an employer.

(10) Manufacturer: The term 'manufacturer' means—

(A) any person who is engaged in a business to produce, create, make, or construct any product (or component part of a product), and who designs or formulates the product (or component part of the product), or has engaged another person to design or formulate the product (or component part of the product);

(B) a product seller, but only with respect to those aspects of a product (or component part of a product) which are created or affected when, before placing the product in the stream of commerce, the product seller produces, creates, makes, constructs, designs, or formulates, or has engaged another person to design or formulate, an aspect of a product (or component part of a product) made by another person; or

(C) any product seller that is not described in subparagraph (B) that holds itself out as a manufacturer to the user of the product.

(11) Noneconomic loss: The term 'noneconomic loss'—

(A) means subjective, nonmonetary loss resulting from harm, including pain, suffering, inconvenience, mental suffering, emotional distress, loss of society and companionship, loss of consortium, injury to reputation, and humiliation; and

(B) does not include economic loss.

(12) Person: The term 'person' means any individual, corporation, company, association, firm, partnership, society, joint stock company, or any other entity (including any governmental entity).

(13) Product:

(A) In general: The term 'product' means any object, substance, mixture, or raw material in a gaseous, liquid, or solid state that—

(i) is capable of delivery itself or as an assembled whole, in a mixed or combined state, or as a component part or ingredient;

(ii) is produced for introduction into trade or commerce;

(iii) has intrinsic economic value; and

(iv) is intended for sale or lease to persons for commercial or personal use.

(B) Exclusion: The term 'product' does not include—

(i) tissue, organs, blood, and blood products used for therapeutic or medical purposes, except to the extent that such tissue, organs, blood, and blood products (or the provision thereof) are subject, under applicable State law, to a standard of liability other than negligence; and

(ii) electricity, water delivered by a utility, natural gas, or steam.

(14) Product liability action: The term 'product liability action' means a civil action brought on any theory for harm caused by a product.

(15) Product seller:

(A) In general: The term 'product seller' means a person who—

(i) in the course of a business conducted for that purpose, sells, distributes, rents, leases, prepares, blends, packages, labels, or otherwise is involved in placing a product in the stream of commerce; or

(ii) installs, repairs, refurbishes, reconditions, or maintains the harm-causing aspect of the product.

(B) Exclusion: The term 'product seller' does not include—

(i) a seller or lessor of real property;

(ii) a provider of professional services in any case in which the sale or use of a product is incidental to the transaction and the essence of the transaction is the furnishing of judgment, skill, or services; or

(iii) any person who—

(I) acts in only a financial capacity with respect to the sale of a product; or

(II) leases a product under a lease arrangement in which the lessor does not initially select the leased product and does not during the lease term ordinarily control the daily operations and maintenance of the product.

(16) State: The term 'State' means each of the several States of the United States, the District of Columbia, the Commonwealth of Puerto Rico, the Virgin Islands, Guam, American Samoa, and the Commonwealth of the Northern Mariana Islands, and any other territory or possession of the United States, or any political subdivision thereof.

(17) Time of delivery: The term 'time of delivery' means the time when a product is delivered to the first purchaser or lessee of the product that was not involved in manufacturing or selling the product, or using the product as a component part of another product to be sold.

SEC. 102. APPLICABILITY; PREEMPTION.

(A) Applicability:

(1) Actions covered: Subject to paragraph (2), this title applies to any product liability action commenced on or after the date of enactment of this Act, without regard to whether the harm that is the subject of the action or the conduct that caused the harm occurred before such date of enactment.

(2) Actions excluded:

(a) Actions for damage to product or commercial loss: A civil action brought for loss or damage to a product itself or for commercial loss, shall not be subject to the provisions of this title governing product liability actions, but shall be subject to any applicable commercial or contract law.

(b) Actions for negligent entrustment: A civil action for negligent entrustment shall not be subject to the provisions of this title governing product liability actions, but shall be subject to any applicable State law.

(B) Scope of Preemption:

(1) In general: This Act supersedes a State law only to the extent that State law applies to an issue covered under this title.

(2) Issues not covered under this act: Any issue that is not covered under this title, including any standard of liability applicable to a manufacturer, shall not be subject to this title, but shall be subject to applicable Federal or State law.

(C) Statutory Construction: Nothing in this title may be construed to—

(1) waive or affect any defense of sovereign immunity asserted by any State under any law;

(2) supersede or alter any Federal law;

(3) waive or affect any defense of sovereign immunity asserted by the United States;

(4) affect the applicability of any provision of chapter 97 of title 28, United States Code;

(5) preempt State choice-of-law rules with respect to claims brought by a foreign nation or a citizen of a foreign nation;

(6) affect the right of any court to transfer venue or to apply the law of a foreign nation or to dismiss a claim of a foreign nation or of a citizen of a foreign nation on the ground of inconvenient forum; or

(7) supersede or modify any statutory or common law, including any law providing for an action to abate a nuisance, that authorizes a person to institute an action for civil damages or civil penalties, cleanup costs, injunctions, restitution, cost recovery, punitive damages, or any other form of relief for remediation of the environment (as defined in Section 101(8) of the Comprehensive Environmental Response, Compensation, and Liability Act of 1980, 42 U.S.C. 9601(8)) or the threat of such remediation.

(D) Construction: To promote uniformity of law in the various jurisdictions, this title shall be construed and applied after consideration of its legislative history.

(E) Effect of Court of Appeals Decisions: Notwithstanding any other provision of law, any decision of a circuit court of appeals interpreting a provision of this title (except to the extent that the decision is overruled or otherwise modified by the Supreme Court) shall be considered a precedent with respect to any subsequent decision made concerning the interpretation of such provision by any Federal or State court within the geographical boundaries of the area under the jurisdiction of the circuit court of appeals.

SEC. 103. ALTERNATIVE DISPUTE RESOLUTION PROCEDURES.

(A) Service of Offer: A claimant or a defendant in a product liability action that is subject to this title may, not later than 60 days after the service of the initial complaint of the claimant or the applicable deadline for a responsive pleading (whichever is later), serve upon an adverse party an offer to proceed pursuant to any voluntary, nonbinding alternative dispute resolution procedure established or recognized under the law of the State in which the product liability action is brought or under the rules of the court in which such action is maintained.

(B) Written Notice of Acceptance or Rejection: Except as provided in subsection (c), not later than 10 days after the service of an offer to proceed under subsection (a), an offeree shall file a written notice of acceptance or rejection of the offer.

(C) Extension: The court may, upon motion by an offeree made prior to the expiration of the 10-day period specified in subsection (b), extend the period for filing a written notice under such subsection for a period of not more than 60 days after the date of expiration of the period specified in subsection (b). Discovery may be permitted during such period.

SEC. 104. LIABILITY RULES APPLICABLE TO PRODUCT SELLERS.

(A) General Rule:

(1) In general: In any product liability action that is subject to this title filed by a claimant for harm caused by a product, a product seller other than a manufacturer shall be liable to a claimant, only if the claimant establishes—

(a) that—

(i) the product that allegedly caused the harm that is the subject of the complaint was sold, rented, or leased by the product seller;

(ii) the product seller failed to exercise reasonable care with respect to the product; and

(iii) the failure to exercise reasonable care was a proximate cause of harm to the claimant; or

(b) that—

(i) the product seller made an express warranty applicable to the product that allegedly caused the harm that is the subject of the complaint, independent of any express warranty made by a manufacturer as to the same product;

(ii) the product failed to conform to the warranty; and

(iii) the failure of the product to conform to the warranty caused harm to the claimant; or

(c) that—

(i) the product seller engaged in intentional wrongdoing, as determined under applicable State law; and

(ii) such intentional wrongdoing w-1Bas a proximate cause of the harm that is the subject of the complaint.

(2) Reasonable opportunity for inspection: For purposes of paragraph (1)(A)(ii), a product seller shall not be considered to have failed to exercise reasonable care with respect to a product based upon an alleged failure to inspect a product if the product seller had no reasonable opportunity to inspect the product that allegedly caused harm to the claimant.

(B) Special Rule:

(1) In general: A product seller shall be deemed to be liable as a manufacturer of a product for harm caused by the product if—

(a) the manufacturer is not subject to service of process under the laws of any State in which the action may be brought; or

(b) the court determines that the claimant would be unable to enforce a judgment against the manufacturer.

(2) Statute of limitations: For purposes of this subsection only, the statute of limitations applicable to claims asserting liability of a product seller as a manufacturer shall be tolled from the date of the filing of a complaint against the manufacturer to the date that judgment is entered against the manufacturer.

(C) Rented or Leased Products:

(1) Notwithstanding any other provision of law, any person engaged in the business of renting or leasing a product (other than a person excluded from the definition of product seller under section 101

(14)(B)) shall be subject to liability in a product liability action under subsection (a), but any person engaged in the business of renting or leasing a product shall not be liable to a claimant for the tortious act of another solely by reason of ownership of such product.

(2) For purposes of paragraph (1), and for determining the applicability of this title to any person subject to paragraph (1), the term 'product liability action' means a civil action brought on any theory for harm caused by a product or product use.

SEC. 105. DEFENSES INVOLVING INTOXICATING ALCOHOL OR DRUGS.

(A) General Rule: Notwithstanding any other provision of law, a defendant in a product liability action that is subject to this title shall have a complete defense in the action if the defendant proves that-

(1) the claimant was under the influence of intoxicating alcohol or any drug that may not lawfully be sold over-the-counter without a prescription, and was not prescribed by a physician for use by the claimant; and

(2) the claimant, as a result of the influence of the alcohol or drug, was more than 50 percent responsible for the accident or event which resulted in the harm to the claimant.

(B) Construction: For purposes of this section, the determination of whether a person was intoxicated or was under the influence of intoxicating alcohol or any drug shall be made pursuant to applicable State law.

SEC. 106. REDUCTION FOR MISUSE OR ALTERATION OF PRODUCT.

(A) General Rule:

(1) In general: Except as provided in subsection (c), in a product liability action that is subject to this title, the damages for which a defendant is otherwise liable under applicable State law shall be reduced by the percentage of responsibility for the harm to the claimant attributable to misuse or alteration of a product by any person if the defendant establishes that such percentage of the harm was proximately caused by a use or alteration of a product—

(a) in violation of, or contrary to, the express warnings or instructions of the defendant if the warnings or instructions are determined to be adequate pursuant to applicable State law; or

(b) involving a risk of harm which was known or should have been known by the ordinary person who uses or consumes the product with the knowledge common to the class of persons who used or would be reasonably anticipated to use the product.

(2) Use intended by a manufacturer is not misuse or alteration: For the purposes of this title, a use of a product that is intended by the manufacturer of the product does not constitute a misuse or alteration of the product.

(B) State Law: Notwithstanding section 3(b), subsection (a) of this section shall supersede State law concerning misuse or alteration of a product only to the extent that State law is inconsistent with such subsection.

(C) Workplace Injury: Notwithstanding subsection (a), the amount of damages for which a defendant is otherwise liable under State law shall not be reduced by the application of this section with respect to the conduct of any employer or coemployee of the plaintiff who is, under applicable State law concerning workplace injuries, immune from being subject to an action by the claimant.

SEC . 107. UNIFORM STANDARDS FOR AWARD OF PUNITIVE DAMAGES.

(A) General Rule: Punitive damages may, to the extent permitted by applicable State law, be awarded against a defendant in a product liability action that is subject to this title if the claimant establishes by clear and convincing evidence that the harm that is the subject of the action was the result of conduct that was carried out by the defendant with a conscious, flagrant indifference to the safety of others.

(B) Limitation on Amount:

(1) In general: Except as provided in paragraphs (2) and (3), the amount of punitive damages that may be awarded to a claimant in a product liability action that is subject to this title shall not exceed the greater of—

(a) 2 times the sum of—

(i) the amount awarded to the claimant for economic loss; and

(ii) the amount awarded to the claimant for noneconomic loss; or

(b) $250,000.

(2) Special rule: The amount of punitive damages that may be awarded in a product liability action that is subject to this title against an individual whose net worth does not exceed $500,000 or against an owner of an unincorporated business, or any partnership,

corporation, association, unit of local government, or organization which has fewer than 25 full-time employees, shall not exceed the lesser of—

(a) 2 times the sum of—

(i) the amount awarded to the claimant for economic loss; and

(ii) the amount awarded to the claimant for noneconomic loss; or

(b) $250,000.

(3) Exception:

(a) Determination by court: Notwithstanding subparagraph (C), in a product liability action that is subject to this title, if the court makes a determination, after considering each of the factors in subparagraph (B), that the application of paragraph (1) would result in an award of punitive damages that is insufficient to punish the egregious conduct of the defendant against whom the punitive damages are to be awarded or to deter such conduct in the future, the court shall determine the additional amount of punitive damages in excess of the amount determined in accordance with paragraph (1) to be awarded to the claimant (referred to in this paragraph as the 'additur') in a separate proceeding in accordance with this paragraph.

(b) Factors for consideration: In any proceeding under subparagraph (A), the court shall consider—

(i) the extent to which the defendant acted with actual malice;

(ii) the likelihood that serious harm would arise from the misconduct of the defendant;

(iii) the degree of the awareness of the defendant of that likelihood;

(iv) the profitability of the misconduct to the defendant;

(v) the duration of the misconduct and any concurrent or subsequent concealment of the conduct by the defendant;

(vi) the attitude and conduct of the defendant upon the discovery of the misconduct and whether the misconduct has terminated;

(vii) the financial condition of the defendant; and

(viii) the cumulative deterrent effect of other losses, damages, and punishment suffered by the defendant as a result of the misconduct, reducing the amount of punitive damages on the basis of the economic impact and severity of all measures to which the defendant has been or may be subjected, including—

(I) compensatory and punitive damage awards to similarly situated claimants;

(II) the adverse economic effect of stigma or loss of reputation;

(III) civil fines and criminal and administrative penalties; and

(IV) stop sale, cease and desist, and other remedial or enforcement orders.

(c) Requirements for awarding additurs: If the court awards an additur under this paragraph, the court shall state its reasons for setting the amount of the additur in findings of fact and conclusions of law. If the additur is—

(i) accepted by the defendant, it shall be entered by the court as a final judgment;

(ii) accepted by the defendant under protest, the order may be reviewed on appeal; or

(iii) not accepted by the defense, the court shall set aside the punitive damages award and order a new trial on the issue of punitive damages only, and judgment shall enter upon the verdict of liability and damages after the issue of punitive damages is decided.

(4) Application by court: This subsection shall be applied by the court and the application of this subsection shall not be disclosed to the jury.

(5) Remittiturs: Nothing in this subsection shall modify or reduce the ability of courts to order remittiturs.

(C) Bifurcation at Request of Any Party:

(1) In general: At the request of any party, the trier of fact in a product liability action that is subject to this title shall consider in a separate proceeding whether punitive damages are to be awarded for the harm that is the subject of the action and the amount of the award.

(2) Inadmissibility of evidence relative only to a claim of punitive damages in a proceeding concerning compensatory damages: If any

party requests a separate proceeding under paragraph (1), in any proceeding to determine whether the claimant may be awarded compensatory damages, any evidence that is relevant only to the claim of punitive damages, as determined by applicable State law, shall be inadmissible.

SEC . 108. LIABILITY FOR CERTAIN CLAIMS RELATING TO DEATH. In any civil action in which the alleged harm to the claimant is death and, as of the effective date of this Act, the applicable State law provides, or has been construed to provide, for damages only punitive in nature, a defendant may be liable for any such damages without regard to section 107, but only during such time as the State law so provides. This section shall cease to be effective September 1, 1996.

SEC . 109. UNIFORM TIME LIMITATIONS ON LIABILITY.

(A) Statute of Limitations:

(1) In general: Except as provided in paragraph (2) and subsection (b), a product liability action that is subject to this title may be filed not later than 2 years after the date on which the claimant discovered or, in the exercise of reasonable care, should have discovered, the harm that is the subject of the action and the cause of the harm.

(2) Exceptions:

(a) Person with a legal disability: A person with a legal disability (as determined under applicable law) may file a product liability action that is subject to this title not later than 2 years after the date on which the person ceases to have the legal disability.

(b) Effect of stay or injunction: If the commencement of a civil action that is subject to this title is stayed or enjoined, the running of the statute of limitations under this section shall be suspended until the end of the period that the stay or injunction is in effect.

(B) Statute of Repose:

(1) In general: Subject to paragraphs (2) and (3), no product liability action that is subject to this title concerning a product that is a durable good alleged to have caused harm (other than toxic harm) may be filed after the 20-year period beginning at the time of delivery of the product.

(2) State law: Notwithstanding paragraph (1), if pursuant to an applicable State law, an action described in such paragraph is required to be filed during a period that is shorter than the 20-year period

specified in such paragraph, the State law shall apply with respect to such period.

(3) Exceptions:

(a) A motor vehicle, vessel, aircraft, or train that is used primarily to transport passengers for hire shall not be subject to this subsection.

(b) Paragraph (1) does not bar a product liability action against a defendant who made an express warranty in writing as to the safety of the specific product involved which was longer than 20 years, but it will apply at the expiration of that warranty.

(c) Paragraph (1) does not affect the limitations period established by the General Aviation Revitalization Act of 1994 (49 U.S.C. 40101 note).

(C) Transitional Provision Relating to Extension of Period for Bringing Certain Actions: If any provision of subsection (a) or (b) shortens the period during which a product liability action that could be otherwise brought pursuant to another provision of law, the claimant may, notwithstanding subsections (a) and (b), bring the product liability action pursuant to this title not later than 1 year after the date of enactment of this Act.

SEC . 110. SEVERAL LIABILITY FOR NONECONOMIC LOSS.

(A) General Rule: In a product liability action that is subject to this title, the liability of each defendant for noneconomic loss shall be several only and shall not be joint.

(B) Amount of Liability:

(1) In general: Each defendant shall be liable only for the amount of noneconomic loss allocated to the defendant in direct proportion to the percentage of responsibility of the defendant (determined in accordance with paragraph (2)) for the harm to the claimant with respect to which the defendant is liable. The court shall render a separate judgment against each defendant in an amount determined pursuant to the preceding sentence.

(2) Percentage of responsibility: For purposes of determining the amount of noneconomic loss allocated to a defendant under this section, the trier of fact shall determine the percentage of responsibility of each person responsible for the claimant's harm, whether or not such person is a party to the action.

SEC . 111. WORKERS' COMPENSATION SUBROGATION STANDARDS.

(A) General Rule:

(1) Right of subrogation:

(a) In general: An insurer shall have a right of subrogation against a manufacturer or product seller to recover any claimant's benefits relating to harm that is the subject of a product liability action that is subject to this title.

(b) Written notification: To assert a right of subrogation under subparagraph (A), the insurer shall provide written notice to the court in which the product liability action is brought.

(c) Insurer not required to be a party: An insurer shall not be required to be a necessary and proper party in a product liability action covered under subparagraph (A).

(2) Settlements and other legal proceedings:

(a) In general: In any proceeding relating to harm or settlement with the manufacturer or product seller by a claimant who files a product liability action that is subject to this title, an insurer may participate to assert a right of subrogation for claimant's benefits with respect to any payment made by the manufacturer or product seller by reason of such harm, without regard to whether the payment is made—

(i) as part of a settlement;

(ii) in satisfaction of judgment;

(iii) as consideration for a covenant not to sue; or

(iv) in another manner.

(b) Written notification: Except as provided in subparagraph (C), an employee shall not make any settlement with or accept any payment from the manufacturer or product seller without written notification to the employer.

(c) Exemption: Subparagraph (B) shall not apply in any case in which the insurer has been compensated for the full amount of the claimant's benefits.

(3) Harm resulting from action of employer or coemployee:

(a) In general: If, with respect to a product liability action that is subject to this title, the manufacturer or product seller attempts to persuade the trier of fact that the harm to the claimant was caused by the fault of the employer of the claimant or any coemployee of the claimant, the issue of that fault shall be submitted to the trier of fact, but only after the manufacturer or product seller has provided timely written notice to the employer.

(b) Rights of employer:

(i) In general: Notwithstanding any other provision of law, with respect to an issue of fault submitted to a trier of fact pursuant to subparagraph (A), an employer shall, in the same manner as any party in the action (even if the employer is not a named party in the action), have the right to—

(I) appear;

(II) be represented;

(III) introduce evidence;

(IV) cross-examine adverse witnesses; and

(V) present arguments to the trier of fact.

(ii) Last issue: The issue of harm resulting from an action of an employer or coemployee shall be the last issue that is presented to the trier of fact.

(c) Reduction of damages: If the trier of fact finds by clear and convincing evidence that the harm to the claimant that is the subject of the product liability action was caused by the fault of the employer or a coemployee of the claimant—

(i) the court shall reduce by the amount of the claimant's benefits—

(I) the damages awarded against the manufacturer or product seller; and

(II) any corresponding insurer's subrogation lien; and

(ii) the manufacturer or product seller shall have no further right by way of contribution or otherwise against the employer.

(d) Certain rights of subrogation not affected: Notwithstanding a finding by the trier of fact described in subparagraph (C), the insurer shall not lose any right of subrogation related to any—

(i) intentional tort committed against the claimant by a coemployee; or

(ii) act committed by a coemployee outside the scope of normal work practices.

(B) Attorney's Fees: If, in a product liability action that is subject to this section, the court finds that harm to a claimant was not caused by the fault of the employer or a coemployee of the claimant, the manufacturer or product seller shall reimburse the insurer for reasonable attorney's fees and court costs incurred by the insurer in the action, as determined by the court.

SEC . 112. FEDERAL CAUSE OF ACTION PRECLUDED. The district courts of the United States shall not have jurisdiction under section 1331 or 1337 of title 28, United States Code, over any product liability action covered under this title.

TITLE II—BIOMATERIALS ACCESS ASSURANCE

SEC . 201. SHORT TITLE. This title may be cited as the 'Biomaterials Access Assurance Act of 1995'.

SEC . 202. FINDINGS.

Congress finds that—

(1) each year millions of citizens of the United States depend on the availability of lifesaving or life-enhancing medical devices, many of which are permanently implantable within the human body;

(2) a continued supply of raw materials and component parts is necessary for the invention, development, improvement, and maintenance of the supply of the devices;

(3) most of the medical devices are made with raw materials and component parts that—

(A) are not designed or manufactured specifically for use in medical devices; and

(B) come in contact with internal human tissue;

(4) the raw materials and component parts also are used in a variety of nonmedical products;

(5) because small quantities of the raw materials and component parts are used for medical devices, sales of raw materials and component parts for medical devices constitute an extremely small portion of the overall market for the raw materials and medical devices;

(6) under the Federal Food, Drug, and Cosmetic Act (21 U.S.C. 301 et seq.), manufacturers of medical devices are required to demonstrate that the medical devices are safe and effective, including demonstrating that the products are properly designed and have adequate warnings or instructions;

(7) notwithstanding the fact that raw materials and component parts suppliers do not design, produce, or test a final medical device, the suppliers have been the subject of actions alleging inadequate—

(A) design and testing of medical devices manufactured with materials or parts supplied by the suppliers; or

(B) warnings related to the use of such medical devices;

(8) even though suppliers of raw materials and component parts have very rarely been held liable in such actions, such suppliers have ceased supplying certain raw materials and component parts for use in medical devices because the costs associated with litigation in order to ensure a favorable judgment for the suppliers far exceeds the total potential sales revenues from sales by such suppliers to the medical device industry;

(9) unless alternate sources of supply can be found, the unavailability of raw materials and component parts for medical devices will lead to unavailability of lifesaving and life-enhancing medical devices;

(10) because other suppliers of the raw materials and component parts in foreign nations are refusing to sell raw materials or component parts for use in manufacturing certain medical devices in the United States, the prospects for development of new sources of supply for the full range of threatened raw materials and component parts for medical devices are remote;

(11) it is unlikely that the small market for such raw materials and component parts in the United States could support the large investment needed to develop new suppliers of such raw materials and component parts;

(12) attempts to develop such new suppliers would raise the cost of medical devices;

(13) courts that have considered the duties of the suppliers of the raw materials and component parts have generally found that the suppliers do not have a duty—

(A) to evaluate the safety and efficacy of the use of a raw material or component part in a medical device; and

(B) to warn consumers concerning the safety and effectiveness of a medical device;

(14) attempts to impose the duties referred to in subparagraphs (A) and (B) of paragraph (13) on suppliers of the raw materials and component parts would cause more harm than good by driving the suppliers to cease supplying manufacturers of medical devices; and

(15) in order to safeguard the availability of a wide variety of lifesaving and life-enhancing medical devices, immediate action is needed—

(A) to clarify the permissible bases of liability for suppliers of raw materials and component parts for medical devices; and

(B) to provide expeditious procedures to dispose of unwarranted suits against the suppliers in such manner as to minimize litigation costs.

SEC . 203. DEFINITIONS.

As used in this title:

(1) Biomaterials supplier:

(A) In general: The term 'biomaterials supplier' means an entity that directly or indirectly supplies a component part or raw material for use in the manufacture of an implant.

(B) Persons included: Such term includes any person who—

(i) has submitted master files to the Secretary for purposes of premarket approval of a medical device; or

(ii) licenses a biomaterials supplier to produce component parts or raw materials.

(2) Claimant:

(A) In general: The term 'claimant' means any person who brings a civil action, or on whose behalf a civil action is brought, arising from harm allegedly caused directly or indirectly by an implant, including a person other than the individual into whose body, or in contact with whose blood or tissue, the implant is placed, who claims to have suffered harm as a result of the implant.

(B) Action brought on behalf of an estate: With respect to an action brought on behalf or through the estate of an individual into whose body, or in contact with whose blood or tissue the implant is placed, such term includes the decedent that is the subject of the action.

(C) Action brought on behalf of a minor: With respect to an action brought on behalf or through a minor, such term includes the parent or guardian of the minor.

(D) Exclusions: Such term does not include—

(i) a provider of professional services, in any case in which—

(I) the sale or use of an implant is incidental to the transaction; and

(II) the essence of the transaction is the furnishing of judgment, skill, or services; or

(ii) a manufacturer, seller, or biomaterials supplier.

(3) Component part:

(A) In general: The term 'component part' means a manufactured piece of an implant.

(B) Certain components: Such term includes a manufactured piece of an implant that—

(i) has significant nonimplant applications; and

(ii) alone, has no implant value or purpose, but when combined with other component parts and materials, constitutes an implant.

(4) Harm:

(A) In general: The term 'harm' means—

(i) any injury to or damage suffered by an individual;

(ii) any illness, disease, or death of that individual resulting from that injury or damage; and

(iii) any loss to that individual or any other individual resulting from that injury or damage.

(B) Exclusion: The term does not include any commercial loss or loss of or damage to an implant.

(5) Implant: The term 'implant' means—

(A) a medical device that is intended by the manufacturer of the device—

(i) to be placed into a surgically or naturally formed or existing cavity of the body for a period of at least 30 days; or

(ii) to remain in contact with bodily fluids or internal human tissue through a surgically produced opening for a period of less than 30 days; and

(B) suture materials used in implant procedures.

(6) Manufacturer: The term 'manufacturer' means any person who, with respect to an implant—

(A) is engaged in the manufacture, preparation, propagation, compounding, or processing (as defined in section 510(a)(1) of the Federal Food, Drug, and Cosmetic Act (21 U.S.C. 360(a)(1)) of the implant; and

(B) is required—

(i) to register with the Secretary pursuant to section 510 of the Federal Food, Drug, and Cosmetic Act (21 U.S.C. 360) and the regulations issued under such section; and

(ii) to include the implant on a list of devices filed with the Secretary pursuant to section 510(j) of such Act (21 U.S.C. 360(j)) and the regulations issued under such section.

(7) Medical device: The term 'medical device' means a device, as defined in section 201(h) of the Federal Food, Drug, and Cosmetic Act (21 U.S.C. 321(h)).

(8) Raw material: The term 'raw material' means a substance or product that—

(A) has a generic use; and

(B) may be used in an application other than an implant.

(9) Secretary: The term Secretary' means the Secretary of Health and Human Services.

(10) Seller:

(A) In general: The term 'seller' means a person who, in the course of a business conducted for that purpose, sells, distributes, leases, packages, labels, or otherwise places an implant in the stream of commerce.

(B) Exclusions: The term does not include—

(i) a seller or lessor of real property;

(ii) a provider of professional services, in any case in which the sale or use of an implant is incidental to the transaction and the essence of the transaction is the furnishing of judgment, skill, or services; or

(iii) any person who acts in only a financial capacity with respect to the sale of an implant.

SEC. 204. GENERAL REQUIREMENTS; APPLICABILITY; PREEMPTION.

(A) General Requirements:

(1) In general: In any civil action covered by this title, a biomaterials supplier may raise any defense set forth in section 205.

(2) Procedures: Notwithstanding any other provision of law, the Federal or State court in which a civil action covered by this title is pending shall, in connection with a motion for dismissal or judgment based on a defense described in paragraph (1), use the procedures set forth in section 206.

(B) Applicability:

(1) In general: Except as provided in paragraph (2), notwithstanding any other provision of law, this title applies to any civil action brought by a claimant, whether in a Federal or State court, against a manufacturer, seller, or biomaterials supplier, on the basis of any legal theory, for harm allegedly caused by an implant.

(2) Exclusion: A civil action brought by a purchaser of a medical device for use in providing professional services against a manufacturer, seller, or biomaterials supplier for loss or damage to an implant or for commercial loss to the purchaser—

(a) shall not be considered an action that is subject to this title; and

(b) shall be governed by applicable commercial or contract law.

(C) Scope of Preemption:

(1) In general: This title supersedes any State law regarding recovery for harm caused by an implant and any rule of procedure applicable to a civil action to recover damages for such harm only to the extent that this title establishes a rule of law applicable to the recovery of such damages.

(2) Applicability of other laws: Any issue that arises under this title and that is not governed by a rule of law applicable to the recovery of damages described in paragraph (1) shall be governed by applicable Federal or State law.

(D) Statutory Construction: Nothing in this title may be construed—

(1) to affect any defense available to a defendant under any other provisions of Federal or State law in an action alleging harm caused by an implant; or

(2) to create a cause of action or Federal court jurisdiction pursuant to section 1331 or 1337 of title 28, United States Code, that otherwise would not exist under applicable Federal or State law.

SEC . 205. LIABILITY OF BIOMATERIALS SUPPLIERS.

(A) In General:

(1) Exclusion from liability: Except as provided in paragraph (2), a biomaterials supplier shall not be liable for harm to a claimant caused by an implant.

(2) Liability: A biomaterials supplier that—

(a) is a manufacturer may be liable for harm to a claimant described in subsection (b);

(b) is a seller may be liable for harm to a claimant described in subsection (c); and

(c) furnishes raw materials or component parts that fail to meet applicable contractual requirements or specifications may be liable for a harm to a claimant described in subsection (d).

(B) Liability as Manufacturer:

(1) In general: A biomaterials supplier may, to the extent required and permitted by any other applicable law, be liable for harm to a claimant caused by an implant if the biomaterials supplier is the manufacturer of the implant.

(2) Grounds for liability: The biomaterials supplier may be considered the manufacturer of the implant that allegedly caused harm to a claimant only if the biomaterials supplier—

(a)(i) has registered with the Secretary pursuant to section 510 of the Federal Food, Drug, and Cosmetic Act (21 U.S.C. 360) and the regulations issued under such section; and

(ii) included the implant on a list of devices filed with the Secretary pursuant to section 510(j) of such Act (21 U.S.C. 360(j)) and the regulations issued under such section;

(b) is the subject of a declaration issued by theSecretary pursuant to paragraph (3) that states that the supplier, with respect to the implant that allegedly caused harm to the claimant, was required to—

(i) register with the Secretary under section 510 of such Act (21 U.S.C. 360), and the regulations issued under such section, but failed to do so; or

---

(ii) include the implant on a list of devices filed with the Secretary pursuant to section 510(j) of such Act (21 U.S.C. 360(j)) and the regulations issued under such section, but failed to do so; or

(c) is related by common ownership or control to a person meeting all the requirements described in subparagraph (A) or (B), if the court deciding a motion to dismiss in accordance with section 206(c)(3)(B)(i) finds, on the basis of affidavits submitted in accordance with section 206, that it is necessary to impose liability on the biomaterials supplier as a manufacturer because the related manufacturer meeting the requirements of subparagraph (A) or (B) lacks sufficient financial resources to satisfy any judgment that the court feels it is likely to enter should the claimant prevail.

(3) Administrative procedures:

(a) In general: The Secretary may issue a declaration described in paragraph (2)(B) on the motion of the Secretary or on petition by any person, after providing—

(i) notice to the affected persons; and

(ii) an opportunity for an informal hearing.

(b) Docketing and final decision: Immediately upon receipt of a petition filed pursuant to this paragraph, the Secretary shall docket the petition. Not later than 180 days after the petition is filed, the Secretary shall issue a final decision on the petition.

(c) Applicability of statute of limitations: Any applicable statute of limitations shall toll during the period during which a claimant has filed a petition with the Secretary under this paragraph.

(C) Liability as Seller: A biomaterials supplier may, to the extent required and permitted by any other applicable law, be liable as a seller for harm to a claimant caused by an implant if—

(1) the biomaterials supplier—

(a) held title to the implant that allegedly caused harm to the claimant as a result of purchasing the implant after—

(i) the manufacture of the implant; and

(ii) the entrance of the implant in the stream of commerce; and

(b) subsequently resold the implant; or

(2) the biomaterials supplier is related by common ownership or control to a person meeting all the requirements described in paragraph (1), if a court deciding a motion to dismiss in accordance with section 206(c)(3)(B)(i) finds, on the basis of affidavits submitted in accordance with section 206, that it is necessary to impose liability on the biomaterials supplier as a seller because the related manufacturer meeting the requirements of paragraph (1) lacks sufficient financial resources to satisfy any judgment that the court feels it is likely to enter should the claimant prevail.

(D) Liability for Violating Contractual Requirements or Specifications: A biomaterials supplier may, to the extent required and permitted by any other applicable law, be liable for harm to a claimant caused by an implant, if the claimant in an action shows, by a preponderance of the evidence, that—

(1) the raw materials or component parts delivered by the biomaterials supplier either—

(a) did not constitute the product described in the contract between the biomaterials supplier and the person who contracted for delivery of the product; or

(b) failed to meet any specifications that were—

(i) provided to the biomaterials supplier and not expressly repudiated by the biomaterials supplier prior to acceptance of delivery of the raw materials or component parts;

(ii)(I) published by the biomaterials supplier;

(II) provided to the manufacturer by the biomaterials supplier; or

(III) contained in a master file that was submitted by the biomaterials supplier to the Secretary and that is currently maintained by the biomaterials supplier for purposes of premarket approval of medical devices; or

(iii)(I) included in the submissions for purposes of premarket approval or review by the Secretary under section 510, 513, 515, or 520 of the Federal Food, Drug, and Cosmetic Act (21 U.S.C. 360, 360c, 360e, or 360j); and

(II) have received clearance from the Secretary, if such specifications were provided by the manufacturer to the biomaterials supplier and were not expressly repudiated by the biomaterials supplier prior to the acceptance by the manufacturer of delivery of the raw materials or component parts; and

(2) such conduct was an actual and proximate cause of the harm to the claimant.

SEC . 206. PROCEDURES FOR DISMISSAL OF CIVIL ACTIONS AGAINST BIOMATERIALS SUPPLIERS.

(A) Motion To Dismiss: In any action that is subject to this title, a biomaterials supplier who is a defendant in such action may, at any time during which a motion to dismiss may be filed under an applicable law, move to dismiss the action on the grounds that—

(1) the defendant is a biomaterials supplier; and

(2)(a) the defendant should not, for the purposes of—

(i) section 205(b), be considered to be a manufacturer of the implant that is subject to such section; or

(ii) section 205(c), be considered to be a seller of the implant that allegedly caused harm to the claimant; or

(b)(i) the claimant has failed to establish, pursuant to section 205(d), that the supplier furnished raw materials or component parts in violation of contractual requirements or specifications; or

(ii) the claimant has failed to comply with the procedural requirements of subsection (b).

(B) Manufacturer of Implant Shall Be Named a Party: The claimant shall be required to name the manufacturer of the implant as a party to the action, unless—

(1) the manufacturer is subject to service of process solely in a jurisdiction in which the biomaterials supplier is not domiciled or subject to a service of process; or

(2) an action against the manufacturer is barred by applicable law.

(C) Proceeding on Motion To Dismiss: The following rules shall apply to any proceeding on a motion to dismiss filed under this section:

(1) Affidavits relating to listing and declarations:

(a) In general: The defendant in the action may submit an affidavit demonstrating that defendant has not included the implant on a list, if any, filed with the Secretary pursuant to section 510(j) of the Federal Food, Drug, and Cosmetic Act (21 U.S.C. 360(j)).

(b) Response to motion to dismiss: In response to the motion to dismiss, the claimant may submit an affidavit demonstrating that—

(i) the Secretary has, with respect to the defendant and the implant that allegedly caused harm to the claimant, issued a declaration pursuant to section 205(b)(2)(B); or

(ii) the defendant who filed the motion to dismiss is a seller of the implant who is liable under section 205(c).

(2) Effect of motion to dismiss on discovery:

(a) In general: If a defendant files a motion to dismiss under paragraph (1) or (2) of subsection (a), no discovery shall be permitted in connection to the action that is the subject of the motion, other than discovery necessary to determine a motion to dismiss for lack of jurisdiction, until such time as the court rules on the motion to dismiss in accordance with the affidavits submitted by the parties in accordance with this section.

(b) Discovery: If a defendant files a motion to dismiss under subsection (a)(2) on the grounds that the biomaterials supplier did not furnish raw materials or component parts in violation of contractual requirements or specifications, the court may permit discovery, as ordered by the court. The discovery conducted pursuant to this subparagraph shall be limited to issues that are directly relevant to—

(i) the pending motion to dismiss; or

(ii) the jurisdiction of the court.

(3) Affidavits relating status of defendant:

(a) In general: Except as provided in clauses (i) and (ii) of subparagraph (B), the court shall consider a defendant to be a biomaterials supplier who is not subject to an action for harm to a claimant caused by an implant, other than an action relating to liability for a violation of contractual requirements or specifications described in subsection (d).

(b) Responses to motion to dismiss: The court shall grant a motion to dismiss any action that asserts liability of the defendant under subsection (b) or (c) of section 205 on the grounds that the defendant is not a manufacturer subject to such section 205(b) or

THE PRODUCT LIABILITY FAIRNESS ACT

seller subject to section 205(c), unless the claimant submits a valid affidavit that demonstrates that—

(i) with respect to a motion to dismiss contending the defendant is not a manufacturer, the defendant meets the applicable requirements for liability as a manufacturer under section 205(b); or

(ii) with respect to a motion to dismiss contending that the defendant is not a seller, the defendant meets the applicable requirements for liability as a seller under section 205(c).

(4) Basis of ruling on motion to dismiss:

(a) In general: The court shall rule on a motion to dismiss filed under subsection (a) solely on the basis of the pleadings of the parties made pursuant to this section and any affidavits submitted by the parties pursuant to this section.

(b) Motion for summary judgment: Notwithstanding any other provision of law, if the court determines that the pleadings and affidavits made by parties pursuant to this section raise genuine issues as concerning material facts with respect to a motion concerning contractual requirements and specifications, the court may deem the motion to dismiss to be a motion for summary judgment made pursuant to subsection (d).

(D) Summary Judgment:

(1) In general:

(a) Basis for entry of judgment: A biomaterials supplier shall be entitled to entry of judgment without trial if the court finds there is no genuine issue as concerning any material fact for each applicable element set forth in paragraphs (1) and (2) of section 205(d).

(b) Issues of material fact: With respect to a finding made under subparagraph (A), the court shall consider a genuine issue of material fact to exist only if the evidence submitted by claimant would be sufficient to allow a reasonable jury to reach a verdict for the claimant if the jury found the evidence to be credible.

(2) Discovery made prior to a ruling on a motion for summary judgment: If, under applicable rules, the court permits discovery prior to a ruling on a motion for summary judgment made pursuant to this subsection, such discovery shall be limited solely to establishing whether a genuine issue of material fact exists.

(3) Discovery with respect to a biomaterials supplier: A biomaterials supplier shall be subject to discovery in connection with a motion seeking dismissal or summary judgment on the basis of the inapplicability of section 205(d) or the failure to establish the applicable elements of section 205(d) solely to the extent permitted by the applicable Federal or State rules for discovery against nonparties.

(E) Stay Pending Petition for Declaration: If a claimant has filed a petition for a declaration pursuant to section 205(b) with respect to a defendant, and the Secretary has not issued a final decision on the petition, the court shall stay all proceedings with respect to that defendant until such time as the Secretary has issued a final decision on the petition.

(F) Manufacturer Conduct of Proceeding: The manufacturer of an implant that is the subject of an action covered under this title shall be permitted to file and conduct a proceeding on any motion for summary judgment or dismissal filed by a biomaterials supplier who is a defendant under this section if the manufacturer and any other defendant in such action enter into a valid and applicable contractual agreement under which the manufacturer agrees to bear the cost of such proceeding or to conduct such proceeding.

(G) Attorney Fees: The court shall require the claimant to compensate the biomaterials supplier (or a manufacturer appearing in lieu of a supplier pursuant to subsection (f)) for attorney fees and costs, if—

(1) the claimant named or joined the biomaterials supplier; and

(2) the court found the claim against the biomaterials supplier to be without merit and frivolous.

SEC . 207. APPLICABILITY. This title shall apply to all civil actions covered under this title that are commenced on or after the date of enactment of this Act, including any such action with respect to which the harm asserted in the action or the conduct that caused the harm occurred before the date of enactment of this Act.

APPENDIX 2:
SECTION 402—RESTATEMENT OF TORTS 2ND (with American Law Institute (ALI) Comments)

§402A. SPECIAL LIABILITY OF SELLER OF PRODUCT FOR PHYSICAL HARM TO USER OR CONSUMER

(1) One who sells any product in a defective condition unreasonably dangerous to the user or consumer or to his property is subject to liability for physical harm thereby caused to the ultimate user or consumer, or to his property, if

(a) the seller is engaged in the business of selling such a product, and

(b) it is expected to and does reach the user or consumer without substantial change in the condition in which it is sold.

(2) The rule stated in Subsection (1) applies although

(a) the seller has exercised all possible care in the preparation and sale of his product, and

(b) the user or consumer has not brought the product from or entered into any contractual relation with the seller.

ALI Caveat: The Institute expresses no opinion as to whether the rules stated in this Section may not apply:

(1) to harm to persons other than users or consumers;

(2) to the seller of a product expected to be processed or otherwise substantially changed before it reaches the user or consumer; or

(3) to the seller of a component part of a product to be assembled.

ALI Comment:

a. This Section states a special rule applicable to sellers of products. The rule is one of strict liability, making the seller subject to liability to the user or consumer even though he has exercised all possible care in the preparation and sale of the product. The Section is inserted in the Chapter dealing with the negligence liability of suppliers of chattels, for convenience of reference and comparison with other Sections dealing with negligence. The rule stated here is not exclusive, and does not preclude liability based upon the alternative ground of negligence of the seller, where such negligence can be proved.

b. History. Since the early days of the common law those engaged in the business of selling food intended for human consumption have been held to a high degree of responsibility for their products. As long ago as 1266 there were enacted special criminal statutes imposing penalties upon victualers, vintners, brewers, butchers, cooks, and other persons who supplied "corrupt" food and drink. In the earlier part of this century this ancient attitude was reflected in a series of decisions in which the courts of a number of states sought to find some method of holding the seller of food liable to the ultimate consumer even though there was no showing of negligence on the part of the seller. These decisions represented a departure from, and an exception to the general rule that a supplier of chattels was not liable to third persons in the absence of negligence or privity of contract. In the beginning, these decisions displayed considerable ingenuity in evolving more or less fictitious theories of liability to fit the case. The various devices included an agency of the intermediate dealer or another to purchase for the consumer, or to sell for the seller; a theoretical assignment of the seller's warranty to the intermediate dealer; a third party beneficiary contract; and an Implied representation that the food was fit for consumption because it was placed on the market, as well as numerous others. In later years the courts have become more or less agreed upon the theory of a "warranty" from the seller to the consumer, either "running with the goods" by analogy to a covenant running with the land, or made directly to the consumer. Other decisions have indicated that the basis is merely one of strict liability in tort, which is not dependent upon either contract or negligence. Recent decisions, since 1950, have extended this special rule of strict liability beyond the seller of food for human consumption. The first extension was into the closely analogous cases of other products intended for intimate bodily use, where, for example, as in the case of cosmetics, the application to the body of the consumer is external rather than internal. Beginning in 1958 with a Michigan case involving cinder building blocks, a number of recent decisions have discarded any limitation to intimate association with the body, and have extended the rule of strict liability to cover the sale of any product which, if it should prove to be defective, may be expected to cause physical harm to the consumer or his property.

c. On whatever theory, the justification for the strict liability has been said to be that the seller, by marketing his product for use and consumption, has undertaken and assumed a special responsibility toward any member of the consuming public who may be injured by it; that the public has a right to and does expect, in the case of products which it needs and for which it is forced to rely upon the seller, that reputable sellers will stand behind their goods; that public policy demands that the burden of accidental injuries caused by products intended for consumption be placed upon those who market them, and be treated as a cost of production against which liability insurance can be obtained; and that consumer of such products is entitled to the maximum of protection at the hands of someone, and the proper persons to afford it are those who market the products.

d. The rule stated in this Section is not limited to the sale of food for human consumption, or other products for intimate bodily use, although it will obviously include them. It extends to any product sold in the condition, or substantially the same condition, in which it is expected to reach the ultimate user or consumer. Thus the rule stated applies to an automobile, a tire, an airplane, a grinding wheel, a water heater, a gas stove, a power tool, a riveting machine, a chair, and an insecticide. It applies also to products which, if they are defective, may be expected to and do cause only "physical harm" in the form of damage to the user's land or chattels, as in the case of animal food or a herbicide.

e. Normally the rule stated in this Section will be applied to articles which already have undergone some processing before sale, since there is today little in the way of consumer products which will reach the consumer without such processing. The rule is not, however, so limited, and the supplier of poisonous mushrooms which are neither cooked, canned, packaged, nor otherwise treated is subject to the liability here stated.

f. Business of selling. The rule stated in this Section applies to any person engaged in the business of selling products for use or consumption. It therefore applies to any manufacturer of such a product, to any wholesale or retail dealer or distributor, and to the operator of a restaurant. It is not necessary that the seller be engaged solely in the business of selling such products. Thus the rule applies to the owner of a motion picture theater who sells popcorn or ice cream, either for consumption on the premises or in packages to be taken home. The rule does not, however, apply to the occasional seller of food or other such products who is not engaged in that activity as a part of his business. Thus it does not apply to the housewife who, on one occasion, sells to her neighbor a jar of jam or a pound of sugar. Nor does it apply to the owner of an automobile who, on one occasion, sells it to his neighbor, or even sells it to a dealer in used cars, and this even though he is fully aware that the dealer plans to resell it. The basis for the rule is the ancient one of the special responsibility for the safety of the public undertaken by one who enters into the business of supplying human beings with products which may endanger the safety of their persons and property, and the forced reliance upon that undertaking on the part of those who purchase such goods. This basis is lacking in the case of the ordinary individual who makes the isolated sale, and he is not liable to a third person, or even to his buyer, in the absence of his negligence. An analogy may be found in the provision of the Uniform Sales Act, §15, which limits the implied warranty of merchantable quality to sellers who deal in such goods; and in the similar limitation of the Uniform Commercial Code, §2-314, to a seller who is a merchant. This Section is also not intended to apply to sales of the stock of merchants out of the usual course of business, such as execution sales, bankruptcy sales, bulk sales, and the like.

g. Defective condition. The rule stated in this Section applies only where the product is, at the time it leaves the seller's hands, in a condition not contemplated by the ultimate consumer, which will be unreasonably dangerous to him. The seller is not liable when he delivers the product in a safe condition, and subsequent mishandling or other causes make it harmful by the time it is consumed. The burden of proof that the product was in a defective condition at the time that it left the hands of the particular seller is upon the injured plaintiff; and unless evidence can be produced which will support the conclusion that it was then defective, the burden is not sustained. Safe condition at the time of delivery by the seller will, however, include proper packaging, necessary sterilization, and other precautions required to permit the product to remain safe for a normal length of time when handled in a normal manner.

h. A product is not in a defective condition when it is safe for normal handling and consumption. If the injury results from abnormal handling, as where a bottled beverage is knocked against a radiator to remove the cap, or from abnormal preparation for use, as where too much salt is added to food, or from abnormal consumption, as where a child eats too much candy and is made ill, the seller is not liable. Where, however, he has reason to anticipate that danger may result from a particular use, as where a drug is sold which is safe only in limited doses, he may be required to give adequate warning of the danger (see Comment i"), and a product sold without such warning is in a defective condition. The defective condition may arise not only from harmful ingredients, not characteristic of the product itself either as to presence or quantity but also from foreign objects contained in the product, from decay or deterioration before sale, or from the way in which the product is prepared or packed. No reason is apparent for distinguishing between the product itself and the container in which it is supplied; and the two are purchased by the user or consumer as an integrated whole. Where the container is itself dangerous, the product is sold in a defective condition. Thus a carbonated beverage in a bottle which is so weak, or cracked, or jagged at the edges, or bottled under such excessive pressure that it may explode or otherwise cause harm to the person who handles it, is in a defective and dangerous condition. The container cannot logically be separated from the contents when the two are sold as a unit, and the liability stated in this Section arises not only when the consumer drinks the beverage and is poisoned by it, but also when he is injured by the bottle while he is handling it preparatory to consumption.

i. Unreasonably dangerous. The rule stated in this Section applies only where the defective condition of the product makes it unreasonably dangerous to the user or consumer. Many products cannot possibly be made entirely safe for all consumption, and any food or drug necessarily involves some risk of harm, if only from over-consumption. Ordinary sugar is a deadly poison to diabetics, and castor oil found use under Mussolini as an instrument of torture. That is not what is meant by "unreasonably dangerous" in this Section. The article sold must be dangerous to an extent beyond that which would be contemplated by the ordinary consumer who purchases it, with the ordinary knowledge common to the community as to its characteristics. Good whiskey is not unreasonably dangerous merely because it will make some people drunk, and is especially dangerous to alcoholics; but bad whiskey, containing a dangerous amount of fusel oil, is unreasonably dangerous. Good tobacco is not unreasonably dangerous merely because the effects of smoking may be harmful but tobacco containing something like marijuana may be unreasonably dangerous. Good butter is not unreasonably dangerous merely because, if such be the case, it deposits cholesterol in the arteries and leads to heart attacks; but bad butter, contaminated with poisonous fish oil, is unreasonably dangerous.

j. Directions or warning. In order to prevent the product from being unreasonably dangerous, the seller may be required to give directions or warning, on the container, as to its use. The seller may reasonably assume that those with common allergies, as for example to eggs or strawberries, will be aware of them, and he is not required to warn against them. Where, however, the product contains an ingredient to which a substantial number of the population are allergic, and the ingredient is one whose danger is not generally known, or if known is one which the consumer would reasonably not expect to find in the product, the seller is required to give warning against it, if he has knowledge, or by the application of reasonable, developed human skill and foresight should have knowledge, of the presence of the ingredient and the danger. Likewise in the case of poisonous drugs, or those unduly dangerous for other reasons, warning as to use may be required. But a seller is not required to warn with respect to products, or ingredients in them, which are only dangerous, or potentially so, when consumed in excessive quantity, or over a long period of time, when the danger, or potentiality of danger, is generally known and recognized. Again the dangers of alcoholic beverages are an example, as are also those of foods containing such substances as saturated fats, which may over a period of time have a deleterious effect upon the human heart. Where warning is given, the seller may reasonably assume that it will be read and heeded; and a product bearing such a warning, which is safe for use if it is followed, is not in defective condition, nor is it unreasonably dangerous.

k. Unavoidably unsafe products. There are some products which, in the present state of human knowledge, are quite incapable of being made safe for their intended and ordinary use. These are especially common in the field of drugs. An outstanding example is the vaccine for the Pasteur treatment of rabies, which not uncommonly leads to very serious and damaging consequences when it is injected. Since the disease itself invariably leads to a dreadful death, both the marketing and the use of the vaccine are fully justified, notwithstanding the unavoidable high degree of risk which they involve. Such a product, properly prepared, and accompanied by proper directions and warning, is not defective, nor is it unreasonably dangerous. The same is true of many other drugs, vaccines, and the like, many of which for this very reason cannot legally be sold except to physicians, or under the prescription of a physician. It is also true in particular of many new or experimental drugs as to which, because of lack of time and opportunity for sufficient medical experience, there can be no assurance of safety, or perhaps even of purity of ingredients, but such experience as there is justifies the marketing and use of the drug notwithstanding a medically recognizable risk. The seller of such products, again with the qualification that they are properly prepared and marketed, and proper warning is given, where the situation calls for it, is not to be held to strict liability for unfortunate consequences attending their use, merely because he has undertaken to supply the public with an apparently useful and desirable product, attended with a known but apparently reasonable risk.

l. User or consumer. In order for the rule stated in this Section to apply, it is not necessary that the ultimate user or consumer have acquired the product directly from the seller, although the rule applies equally if he does so. He may have acquired it through one or more intermediate dealers. It is not even necessary that the consumer have purchased the product at all. He may be a member of the family of the final purchaser, or his employee, or a guest at his table, or a mere donee from the purchaser. The liability stated is one in tort, and does not require any contractual relation, or privity of contract, between the plaintiff and the defendant. "Consumers" include not only those who in fact consume the product, but also those who prepare it for consumption; and the housewife who contracts tularemia while cooking rabbits for her husband is included within the rule stated in this Section, as is also the husband who is opening a bottle of beer for his wife to drink. Consumption includes all ultimate uses for which the product is intended, and the customer in a beauty shop to whose hair a permanent wave solution is applied by the shop is a consumer. "User" includes those who are passively enjoying the benefit of the product, as in the case of passengers in automobiles or airplanes, as well as those who are utilizing it for the purpose of doing work upon it, as in the case of an employee of the ultimate buyer who is making repairs upon the automobile which he has purchased.

ALI Illustration:

> 1. A manufactures and packs a can of beans, which he sells to B, a wholesaler. B sells the beans to C, a jobber, who resells it to D, a retail grocer. E buys the can of beans from D, and gives it to F. F serves the beans at lunch to C, his guest. While eating the beans, G breaks a tooth, on a pebble of the size, shape, and color of a bean, which no reasonable inspection could possibly have discovered. There is satisfactory evidence that the pebble was in the can of beans when it was opened. Although there is no negligence on the part of A, B, C, or D, each of them is subject to liability to G. On the other hand E and F, who have not

sold the beans, are not liable to G in the absence of some negligence on their part.

m. "Warranty." The liability stated in this Section does not rest upon negligence. It is strict liability, similar in its nature to that covered by Chapters 20 and 21. The basis of liability is purely one of tort. A number of courts, seeking a theoretical basis for the liability, have resorted to a "warranty," either running with the goods sold, by analogy to covenants running with the land, or made directly to the consumer without contract. In some instances this theory has proved to be an unfortunate one. Although warranty was in its origin a matter of tort liability, and it is generally agreed that a tort action will still lie for its breach, it has become so identified in practice with a contract of sale between the plaintiff and the defendant that the warranty theory has become something of an obstacle to the recognition of the strict liability where there is no such contract. There is nothing in this Section which would prevent any court from treating the rule stated as a matter of "warranty" to the user or consumer. But if this is done, it should be recognized and understood that the "warranty" is a very different kind of warranty from those usually found in the sale of goods, and that it is not subject to the various contract rules which have grown up to surround such sales. The rule stated in this Section does not require any reliance on the part of the consumer upon the reputation, skill, or judgment of the seller who is to be held liable, nor any representation or undertaking on the part of that seller. The seller is strictly liable although, as is frequently the case, the consumer does not even know who he is at the time of consumption. The rule stated in this Section is not governed by the provisions of the Uniform Sales Act, or those of the Uniform Commercial Code, as to warranties; and it is not affected by limitations on the scope and content of warranties, or by limitation to "buyer" and "seller" in those statutes. Nor is the consumer required to give notice to the seller of his injury within a reasonable time after it occurs, as is provided by the Uniform Act. The consumer's cause of action does not depend upon the validity of his contract with the person from whom he acquires the product, and it is not affected by any disclaimer or other agreement, whether it be between the seller and his immediate buyer, or attached to and accompanying the product into the consumer's hands. In short, "warranty" must be given a new and different meaning if it is used in connection with this Section. It is much simpler to regard the liability here stated as merely one of strict liability in tort.

n. Contributory negligence. Since the liability with which this Section deals is not based upon negligence of the seller, but is strict liability, the rule applied to strict liability cases (see §524) applies. Contributory negligence of the plaintiff is not a defense when such negligence consists merely in a failure to discover the defect in the product, or to guard against the possibility of its existence. On the other hand the form of contributory negligence which consists in voluntarily and unreasonably proceeding to encounter a known danger, and commonly passes under the name of assumption of risk, is a defense under this Section as in other cases of strict liability. If the user or consumer discovers the defect and is aware of the danger, and nevertheless proceeds unreasonably to make use of the product and is injured by it, he is barred from recovery.

ALI Comment on Caveat:

o. Injuries to nonusers and nonconsumers. Thus far the courts, in applying the rule stated in this Section, have not gone beyond allowing recovery to users and consumers, as those terms are defined in Comment l. Casual bystanders, and others who many come in contact with the product, as in the case of employees of the retailer, or a passerby injured by an exploding bottle, or a pedestrian hit by an automobile, have been denied recovery. There may be no essential reason why such plaintiffs should not be brought within the scope of the protection afforded, other than that they do not have the same reasons for expecting such protection as the consumer who buys a marketed product; but the social pressure which has been largely responsible for the development of the rule stated has been a consumers' pressure, and there is not the same demand for the protection of casual strangers. The Institute expresses neither approval nor disapproval of expansion of the rule to permit recovery by such persons.

p. Further processing or substantial change. Thus far the decisions applying the rule stated have not gone beyond products which are sold in the condition, or in substantially the same condition, in which they are expected to reach the hands of the ultimate user or consumer. In the absence of decisions providing a clue to the rules which are likely to develop, the Institute has refrained from taking any position as to the possible liability of the seller where the product is expected to, and does, undergo further processing or other substantial change after it leaves his hands and before it reaches those of the ultimate user or consumer. It seems reasonably clear that the mere fact that the product is to undergo processing, or other substantial change, will not in all cases relieve the seller of liability under the rule stated in this Section. If, for example, raw coffee beans are sold to a buyer who roasts and packs them for sale to the ultimate consumer, it cannot be supposed that the seller will be relieved of all liability when the raw beans are contaminated with arsenic, or some other poison. Likewise the seller of an automobile with a defective steering gear which breaks and injures the driver, can scarcely expect to be relieved of the responsibility by reason of the fact that the car is sold to a dealer who is expected to "service" it, adjust the brakes, mount and inflate the tires, and the like, before it is ready for use. On the other hand, the manufacturer of pig iron, which is capable of a wide variety of uses, is not so likely to be held to strict liability when it turns out to be unsuitable for the child's tricycle into which it is finally made by a remote buyer. The question is essentially one of whether the responsibility for discovery and prevention of the dangerous defect is shifted to the intermediate party who is to make the changes. No doubt there will be some situations, and some defects, as to which the responsibility will be shifted, and others in which it will not. The existing decisions as yet throw no light upon the questions, and the Institute therefore expresses neither approval nor disapproval of the seller's strict liability in such a case.

q. Component parts. The same problem arises in cases of the sale of a component part of a product to be assembled by another, as for example a tire to be placed on a new automobile, a brake cylinder for the same purpose, or an instrument for the panel of an airplane. Again the question arises, whether the responsibility is not shifted to the assembler. It is no doubt to be expected that where there is no change in the component part itself, but it is merely incorporated into something larger, the strict liability will be found to carry through to the ultimate user or consumer. But in the absence of a sufficient number of decisions on the matter to justify a conclusion, the Institute expresses no opinion on the matter.

§402B. MISREPRESENTATION BY SELLER OF CHATTELS TO CONSUMER

One engaged in the business of selling chattels who, by advertising, labels, or otherwise, makes to the public a misrepresentation of a material fact concerning the character or quality of a chattel sold by him is subject to liability for physical harm to a consumer of the chattel caused by justifiable reliance upon the misrepresentation, even though

(a) it is not made fraudulently or negligently, and

(b) the consumer has not bought the chattel from or entered into any contractual relation with the seller.

ALI Caveat: The Institute expresses no opinion as to whether the rule stated in this Section may apply

(1) where the representation is not made to the public, but to an individual, or

(2) where physical harm is caused to one who is not a consumer of the chattel.

ALI Comment:

a. The rule stated in this Section is one of strict liability for physical harm to the consumer, resulting from a misrepresentation of the character or quality of the chattel sold, even though the misrepresentation is an innocent one, and not made fraudulently or negligently. Although the Section deals with misrepresentation, it is inserted here in order to complete the rules dealing with the liability of suppliers of chattels for physical harm caused by the chattel. A parallel rule, as to strict liability for pecuniary loss resulting from such a misrepresentation, is stated in §552 D.

b. The rule stated in this Section differs from the rule of strict liability stated in §402 A, which is a special rule applicable only to sellers of products for consumption and does not depend upon misrepresentation. The rule here stated applies to one engaged in the business of selling any type of chattel, and is limited to misrepresentations of their character or quality.

e. History. The early rule was that a seller of chattels incurred no liability for physical harm resulting from the use of the chattel to anyone other than his immediate buyer, unless there was privity of contract between them. (See §395, Comment o.) Beginning with Langridge v. Levy, 2 M. & W. 519, 150 Eng. Rep. 863(1837), an exception was developed in cases where the seller made fraudulent misrepresentations to the immediate buyer, concerning the character or quality of the chattel sold, and because of the fact misrepresented harm resulted to a third person who was using the chattel. The remedy lay in an action for deceit, and the rule which resulted is now stated in §557 A. Shortly after 1930, a number of the American courts began, more or less independently, to work out a further extension of liability for physical harm to the consumer of the chattel, in cases where the seller made misrepresentations to the public concerning its character or quality, and the consumer, as a member of the public, purchased the chattel in reliance upon the misrepresentation and suffered physical harm because of the fact misrepresented. In such cases the seller was held to strict liability for the misrepresentation, even though it was not made fraudulently or negligently.

The leading case is Baxter v. Ford Motor Co., 168 Wash. 456, 12 P. 2d 409, 88 A.L.R. 521 (1932), adhered to on rehearing, 168 Wash. 465, 15 P. 2d 118, 88 A.L.R. 527, second appeal, 179 Wash. 123, 35 P. 2d 1090 (1934), in which the manufacturer of an automobile advertised to the public that the windshield glass was "shatterproof," and the purchaser was injured when a stone struck the glass and it shattered. In the beginning various theories of liability were suggested, including strict liability in deceit, and a contract resulting from an offer made to the consumer to be bound by the representation, accepted by his purchase.

d. "Warranty. " The theory finally adopted by most of the decisions, however, has been that of a noncontractual "express warranty" made to the consumer in the form of the representation to the public upon which he relies. The difficulties attending the use of the word "warranty" are the same as those involved under §402 A, and Comment m under that Section is equally applicable here so far as it is pertinent. The liability stated in this Section is liability in tort, and not in contract; and if it is to be called one of "warranty," it is at least a different kind of warranty from that involved in the ordinary sale of goods from the immediate seller to the immediate buyer, and is subject to different rules.

e. Sellers included. The rule stated in this Section applies to any person engaged in the business of selling any type of chattel. It is not limited to sellers of food or products for intimate bodily use, as was until lately the rule stated in §402 A. It is not limited to manufacturers of the chattel, and it includes wholesalers, retailers, and other distributors who sell it. The rule stated applies, however, only to those who are engaged in the business of selling such chattels. It has no application to anyone who is not so engaged in business. It does not apply, for example, to a newspaper advertisement published by a private owner of a single automobile who offers it for sale.

f. Misrepresentation of character or quality. The rule stated applies to any misrepresentation of a material fact concerning the character or quality of the chattel sold which is made to the public by one so engaged in the business of selling such chattels. The fact misrepresented must be a material one, upon which the consumer may be expected to rely in making his purchase, and he must justifiably rely upon it. (See Comment j.) If he does so, and suffers physical harm by reason of the fact misrepresented, there is strict liability to him.

ALI Illustration:

> 1. A manufactures automobiles. He advertises in newspapers and magazines that the glass in his cars is "shatterproof." B reads this advertising, and in reliance upon it purchases from a retail dealer an automobile manufactured by A. While B is driving the car, a stone thrown up by a passing truck strikes the windshield and shatters it, injuring B. A is subject to strict liability to B.

g. Material fact. The rule stated in this Section applies only to misrepresentations of material facts concerning the character or quality of the chattel in question. It does not apply to statements of opinion, and in particular it does not apply to the kind of loose general praise of wares sold which, on the part of the seller, is considered to be "sales talk," and is commonly called "puffing"—as, for example, a statement that an automobile is the best on the market for the price. As to such general language of opinion, see §542, and Comment d under that Section, which is applicable here so far as it is pertinent. In addition, the fact misrepresented must be a material one, of importance to the normal purchaser, by which the ultimate buyer may justifiably be expected to be influenced in buying the chattel.

h. "To the public." The rule stated in this Section is limited to misrepresentations which are made by the seller to the public at large, in order to induce purchase of the chattels sold, or are intended by the seller to, and do, reach the public. The form of the representation is not importance. It may be made by public advertising in newspapers or television, by literature distributed to the public through dealers, by labels on the product sold, or leaflets accompanying it, or in any other manner, whether it be oral or written.

ALI Illustrations:

> 2. A manufactures wire rope. He issues a manual containing statements concerning its strength, which he distributes through dealers to buyers, and to members of the public who may be expected to buy. In reliance upon the statements made in the manual, B buys a quantity of the wire rope from a dealer, and makes use of it to hoist a weight of 1,000 pounds. The strength of the rope is not as great as is represented in the manual, and as a result the rope breaks and the weight falls on B and injures him. A is subject to strict liability to B.

> 3. A manufactures a product for use by women at home in giving "permanent waves" to their hair. He places on the bottles labels which state that the product may safely be used in a

particular manner, and will not be injurious to the hair. B reads such a label, and in reliance upon it purchases a bottle of the product from a retail dealer. She uses it as directed, and as a result her hair is destroyed. A is subject to strict liability to B.

i. Consumers. The rule stated in this Section is limited to strict liability for physical harm to consumers of the chattel. The Caveat leaves open the question whether the rule may not also apply to one who is not a consumer, but who suffers physical harm through his justifiable reliance upon the misrepresentation. "Consumer" is to be understood in the broad sense of one who makes use of the chattel in the manner which a purchaser may be expected to use it. Thus an employee of the ultimate purchaser to whom the chattel is turned over, and who is directed to make use of it in his work, is a consumer, and so is the wife of the purchaser of an automobile who is permitted by him to drive it.

j. Justifiable reliance. The rule here stated applies only where there is justifiable reliance upon the misrepresentation of the seller, and physical harm results because of such reliance, and because of the fact which is misrepresented. It does not apply where the misrepresentation is not known, or there is indifference to it, and it does not influence the purchase or subsequent conduct. At the same time, however, the misrepresentation need not be the sole inducement to purchase, or to use the chattel, and it is sufficient that it has been a substantial factor in that inducement. (Compare §546 and Comments.) Since the liability here is for misrepresentation, the rules as to what will constitute justifiable reliance stated in §§537-545 A are applicable to this Section, so far as they are pertinent. The reliance need not necessarily be that of the consumer who is injured. It may be that of the ultimate purchaser of the chattel, who because of such reliance passes it on to the consumer who is in fact injured, but is ignorant of the misrepresentation. Thus a husband who buys an automobile in justifiable reliance upon statements concerning its brakes, and permits his wife to drive the car, supplies the element of reliance, even though the wife in fact never learns of the statements.

ALI Illustration:

4. The same facts as in Illustration 2, except that the harm is suffered by C, an employee of B, to whom B turns over the wire rope without informing him of the representations made by A. The same result.

APPENDIX 3:
CASE INFORMATION CHECKLIST IN A
PRODUCT LIABILITY ACTION

SECTION ONE: BACKGROUND OF INJURED PARTY

1. Name and address.

2. Age.

3. Gender.

4. Occupation and salary.

5. Proof of loss of earnings.

6. Highest level of education.

7. Marital status.

8. Names and addresses of immediate family members.

9. Obtain complete medical history and obtain and review all medical records both before and after occurrence, review nature and scope of injury and prognosis.

10. Documentation of medical bills and related costs.

SECTION TWO: SPECIFICS OF OCCURRENCE

1. Describe all steps leading up to injury.

2. Detailed description of how injury occurred.

3. Date and time of occurrence.

4. Was possibility of occurrence discussed in any instructions, manuals, or warnings?

5. Was product being used according to instructions? Any deviations?

6. Identify witnesses and obtain statements.

7. Identify and obtain copies of any official reports, e.g. police reports, news reports, etc.

SECTION THREE: PRODUCT IDENTIFICATION

Chain of Distribution

1. Manufacturer:

2. Manufacturers of component parts:

3. Assemblers:

4. Wholesalers:

5. Distributors:

6. Retailers:

7. Others:

Product History

1. Age of product including date of manufacture.

2. Was product purchased new, used or reconditioned?

3. Life expectancy of product.

4. Effects of normal wear and tear on product.

5. Maintenance history of product.

SECTION FOUR: ACQUISITION OF PRODUCT

1. Preserve product.

2. Note physical description of product.

3. Photographs of product.

4. Product packaging. Note any printing on packaging.

5. Product labels. Note any printing on labels.

6. Product instructions and manuals.

7. Check for warnings on product labels, instructions or packaging.

8. Sales receipt, invoice or contract.

9. Other identifying information, e.g. serial number, model number, etc.

10. Copies of any correspondence concerning product.

SECTION FIVE: PRODUCT WARRANTIES

1. Relationship between injured party and purchaser if not the same.

2. Did purchaser inspect product prior to purchase?

3. Did purchaser make known to seller any particular use or other requirement of product.

4. State specific words spoken by seller to purchaser as inducement for sale.

5. Was there reliance on seller's statements by purchaser.

6. Copies of written warranties or guarantees, if any.

7. Determine whether there exist any disclaimers or limitations on warranties.

8. Obtain existence of advertising, e.g., radio and television; newspaper; magazine, etc.

SECTION SIX: PRODUCT TESTING

1. Obtain duplicate product for comparison testing.

2. Obtain expert to perform testing.

3. Obtain design information, e.g patent files, specification sheets, modifications, consultants, etc.

SECTION SEVEN: DETERMINATION OF DEFECT

1. Describe intended use of product.

2. Describe all other known or common uses of product.

3. Describe all possible uses of product.

4. How is product designed to operate?

5. How was product being used at time of injury?

6. Is product dangerous?

7. Are there safer alternatives to accomplish task?

8. Determine existence of regulations, e.g. State and Federal regulations.

9. Determine existence of standards, e.g. state of the art and industry standards.

APPENDIX 4:
SAMPLE PRODUCT LIABILITY
COMPLAINT—DEFECTIVE PRODUCT

[NAME OF COURT]

[CAPTION OF CASE] [FILE INDEX NUMBER]

COMPLAINT

Plaintiff, by his attorney, [name of attorney], complaining of the defendant, alleges, as follows:

FIRST: Plaintiff is a resident of the City, County and State of New York.

SECOND: Upon information and belief at all times hereinafter mentioned the defendant was and still is a domestic corporation, duly organized and existing under and by virtue of the laws of the State of New York.

FOR A FIRST CAUSE OF ACTION

THIRD: Upon information and belief, the defendant corporation is, and for approximately 10 years prior to March 7th, 2000, has been, engaged in the business of the manufacture and sale of bicycles to ultimate consumers such as the plaintiff and did, in fact, manufacture the bicycle owned and operated by the plaintiff.

FOURTH: Defendant designed, tested, manufactured, sold and promoted the bicycle, known as Model Number XZY123.

FIFTH: On March 7, 2000, plaintiff purchased one of defendant's bicycles, known as Model Number XYZ123.

SIXTH: On July 4, 2000, plaintiff was operating this bicycle when the handle bars cracked and dislodged from the main frame of the bicycle.

SEVENTH: Defendant was careless in the design, testing, inspection, manufacture, distribution, labeling, sale and promotion of said bicycle.

EIGHTH: As a result of defendant's conduct, plaintiff was seriously injured and has sustained general and special damages.

SECOND CAUSE OF ACTION

NINTH: Plaintiff repeats and reiterates each allegation contained in paragraphs 1 through 8 of this complaint.

TENTH: The bicycle was defective in that the handlebars broke and dislodged from the main frame as a result of which defendant has become strictly liable to plaintiff.

ELEVENTH: By reason of the foregoing, the plaintiff has been damaged in the sum of One Hundred Fifty ($150,000) Dollars.

WHEREFORE, plaintiff demands judgment against defendant in the amount of One Hundred Fifty ($150,000) Dollars; costs and disbursements of this action; and any other relief the Court deems appropriate.

PLEASE TAKE NOTICE, that pursuant to the [cite applicable rules of Court], you are required to serve a copy of your answer within 20 days after the service of this Complaint.

Dated:

[Signature Line]

[Name of Attorney]

Attorney for Plaintiff

[Attorney's Address]

[Attorney's Telephone Number]

APPENDIX 5:
STATE WRONGFUL DEATH STATUTES

JURISDICTION	STATUTE
Alabama	Code of Alabama § 10-5-410
Alaska	Alaska Statutes § 09.55.580
Arizona	Arizona Revised Statutes § 12-542
Arkansas	Arkansas Statutes Annotated § 27-906
California	California Code of Civil Procedure § 377
Colorado	Colorado Revised Statutes § 13-21-201
Connecticut	Connecticut General Statutes Annotated § 52-555
Delaware	Delaware Code Annotated Title 10 § 3701
District of Columbia	District of Columbia Code Title 16 § 2702
Florida	Florida Statutes Annotated § 768.20
Georgia	Code of Georgia § 51-4-2
Hawaii	Hawaii Revised Statutes § 666-3
Idaho	Idaho Code § 5-310
Illinois	Illinois Revised Statutes Chapter 70 § 2
Indiana	Indiana Code Annotated § 34-4-2-1
Iowa	Code of Iowa § 611.20
Kansas	Kansas Statutes § 60-1902
Kentucky	Kentucky Revised Statutes § 411.130
Louisiana	Louisiana Revised Statutes § 2315
Maine	Maine Revised Statutes Annotated Title 18A § 2-804
Maryland	Maryland Courts & Judicial Procedure Code Annotated § 3-904

JURISDICTION	STATUTE
Massachusetts	Annotated Laws of Massachusetts Chapter 229 § 2
Michigan	Michigan Compiled Laws § 600.2922
Minnesota	Minnesota Statutes § 573.02
Mississippi	Mississippi Code Annotated § 11-7-13
Missouri	Annotated Missouri Statutes § 537.080
Montana	Revised Montana Code Annotated § 27-1-512
Nebraska	Revised Statutes of Nebraska § 30-810
Nevada	Nevada Revised Statutes § 41.080
New Hampshire	New Hampshire Revised Statutes Annotated § 556:12
New Jersey	New Jersey Statutes Annotated § 2A:31-1
New Mexico	New Mexico Statutes Annotated § 41-2-1
New York	New York EPTL § 5-4.1
North Carolina	General Statutes of North Carolina § 28A-18-2
North Dakota	North Dakota Century Code § 32-21-03
Ohio	Ohio Revised Code Annotated § 2125.02
Oklahoma	Oklahoma Statutes Annotated Title 12 § 1053
Oregon	Oregon Revised Statutes § 30.020
Pennsylvania	Pennsylvania Statutes Annotated Title 42 § 8301
Rhode Island	General Laws of Rhode Island § 10-7-2
South Carolina	Code of Laws of South Carolina § 15-51-20
South Dakota	South Dakota Codified Laws Annotated § 21-5-5
Tennessee	Tennessee Code Annotated § 20-5-106
Texas	Texas Revised Civil Statutes Annotated Article 5525
Utah	Utah Code Annotated § 78-11-6
Vermont	Vermont Statutes Annotated Title 14 § 1491
Virginia	Code of Virginia Annotated § 8.01-56
Washington	Washington Revised Code Annotated § 4.20.010
West Virginia	West Virginia Code § 55-7-6

APPENDIX 6:
SETTLEMENT AGREEMENT AND MUTUAL
RELEASE OF CLAIMS

AGREEMENT made as of the ____ day of December, 2001, between JOHN DOE, [address] (hereinafter "Doe") and ABC Corporation, [address] (hereinafter, "Manufacturer").

IN CONSIDERATION of the mutual covenants and agreements herein contained, the parties hereto agree as follows:

1. In full, final and complete settlement of any and all claims, as provided hereinbelow, and upon execution of this Agreement by the parties, Manufacturer agrees to pay Doe the total sum of Twenty Five Thousand ($25,000) Dollars by check, subject to collection.

2. Doe hereby releases and forever discharges Manufacturer, its affiliated organizations, and its officers, directors, trustees, employees, agents, attorneys, successors and heirs, from any and all claims arising out of or in connection with any acts or omissions by Manufacturer.

3. Specifically, Doe releases Manufacturer from any and all claims resulting from physical injuries sustained as a result of the use of a product known as the E-Z Box Cutter.

4. The parties agree to keep the terms of this settlement, and the allegations giving rise to this Agreement, completely confidential, and will not hereinafter disclose any information concerning them to anyone, including any newspaper, magazine, radio or television station, or any other media, or any agents, employees or representatives of such media.

5. This Agreement shall be binding upon, and inure to the benefit of, each of the parties to this Agreement, and upon their respective heirs, administrators, representatives, executors and successors, if any.

6. This Agreement constitutes the entire agreement between the parties hereto and supersedes any and all other agreements, understandings, negotiations, or discussions, either oral or in writing, express or implied between the parties hereto.

7. This Agreement may not be amended, altered, modified or otherwise changed, except in a writing executed by the parties hereto.

IN WITNESS WHEREOF, the parties hereto have caused this agreement to be executed as of the date above set forth.

DATED:

BY: _____
                JOHN DOE

DATED:

THE E-Z BOX CUTTER MANUFACTURING CO.

BY: _____
            MARY SMITH, IT'S PRESIDENT

APPENDIX 7:
SAMPLE RETAINER AGREEMENT IN A
PRODUCT LIABILITY LAWSUIT

RETAINER AGREEMENT

DATED this 1st day of December, 2001, the undersigned, Mr. John Doe ("Client"), retains and employs Mary Jones, Esq. ("Attorney") as his Attorney to represent him with full authorization to do all things necessary to investigate and prosecute his claims against any and all responsible parties relating to a personal injury action arising out of an accident which occurred on or about December 1, 2000.

The undersigned agrees to the following terms and conditions:

1. Client hereby gives Attorney the exclusive right to take all legal steps to enforce this claim through trial and appeal. The attorney shall have the right but not the obligation to represent Client on appeal. If appellate litigation becomes necessary, a new retainer agreement will be required prior to attorney representing client in such litigation.

2. Attorney has agreed to take client's case on a contingency fee basis. This means that attorney's legal fees will be paid only if client receives a monetary judgment or settlement in this matter. Attorney will receive no fee if there is no recovery. In consideration of the services rendered and to be rendered, the contingency fee in this matter will be one-third of any amount recovered by settlement or judgment.

3. In addition, it may be necessary for Attorney to advance certain out-of-pocket expenses during the course of litigation. Client agrees to reimburse Attorney for any such expenses advanced on his behalf. Such expenses, to the extent that they have not been prepaid, shall be subtracted from any sum recovered after the attorney fee is deducted.

4. Attorney acknowledges that a retainer in the amount of [$xxx] has been received from Client to be applied against actual out-of-pocket expenses, as they accrue. A statement of expenses shall be sent to Client on demand.

5. If the cause of action is settled by client without the consent of Attorney, Client agrees to pay Attorney the above percentage of the full amount of the settlement for the benefit of Client, to whomever paid. The Attorney shall have, in the alternative, the option of seeking compensation on a *quantum meruit* basis to be determined by the Court. In such circumstances, the court would determine the fair value of the services rendered, in addition to taxable costs and disbursements.

6. If Attorney is terminated by client prior to resolution of this matter, client agrees to pay all legal fees and costs incurred for services rendered on client's behalf thus far, at Attorney's hourly rate, which is currently [$xxx] per hour, unless both Attorney and Client agree, in writing, to other payment arrangements prior to such termination.

7. Client understands and agrees that Attorney cannot commence work in this matter until this agreement is signed and returned to Attorney's office. By signing below where indicated, Client acknowledges that he has received a copy of this retainer letter , and understands and agrees to its terms and conditions.

ACCEPTED BY: _____
John Doe, Client

The above employment is hereby accepted on the terms stated.

ACCEPTED BY: _____
Mary Jones, Attorney

APPENDIX 8:
SAMPLE PRODUCT SAFETY RECALL NOTICE

NEWS FROM CPSC

U.S. CONSUMER PRODUCT SAFETY COMMISSION

Office of Information and Public Affairs   Washington, DC 20207

FOR IMMEDIATE RELEASE

October 09, 2001

Release # 02-006

Bike Rim Recall Hotline: (877) 887-2572

CPSC CONTACT: Kim Dulic

(301) 504-0580 Ext. 1183

CPSC, SALSA CYCLES ANNOUNCE RECALL OF BICYCLE RIMS

WASHINGTON, D.C.– In cooperation with the U.S. Consumer Product Safety Commission (CPSC), Salsa Cycles, of Bloomington, Minn., is voluntarily recalling about 500 disc-brake specific bicycle rims. The rims can unexpectedly fail during normal use, posing the risk of falls and serious injury to riders. Salsa Cycles has received six reports of rims failing during use; though, no injuries have been reported. The recalled rims are the Salsa Alto models, which have a black anodized finish and are labeled "Salsa" and "Salsa Alto" in yellow, red and white. The rims, which are used on mountain bikes that have disc brakes, were sold individually or built up into wheels with Shimano Deore or Deore XT hubs. Independent bicycle dealers sold these rims from January 2001 through August 2001 for $50 (individually) or between $100 and $150 (in built up wheels). Consumers with the recalled rims should stop using them immediately and return them to the store where purchased, for a full refund or free replacement.

APPENDIX 9:
SAMPLE CONSUMER PRODUCT INCIDENT REPORT

U.S. CONSUMER PRODUCT SAFETY COMMISSION

CONSUMER PRODUCT INCIDENT REPORT

By filling out the form below and then submitting it, you can report any injury or death involving consumer products to us, or report an unsafe product to us. We may contact you by mail, phone or Internet email for further details. In addition, you will be contacted to confirm the information you sent. Please provide as much information as possible. Your name, address, and telephone number are optional, but we can't contact you without that information. You can also report an incident or unsafe product by calling toll-free at 1-800-638-2772.

The CPSC does not have jurisdiction over automobiles, trucks and motorcycles, car seats protecting children in on-road vehicles, foods, medicines, cosmetics, and medical devices, or dissatisfaction with business practices.

Your name:

Your address:

City:

State:

Zip code:

E-mail address:

Your telephone:

Name of victim (if different from above):

Victim address:

City:

State:

Zip code:

Victim telephone:

Describe the incident or hazard, including description of injuries

Victim's age at time of incident:

Victim's sex:

[ ] Female

[ ] Male

Date of Incident:

Describe product involved:

Product Brand Name/Manufacturer:

Place where manufactured (City and State):

Do you still have the product?

[ ] Yes

[ ] No

Product model and serial number:

When was the product purchased?

May we use your name with this report?

[ ] I request that you do not release my name.

[ ] You may release my name to the manufacturer but I request that you do not release it to the general public.

[ ] You may release my name to the manufacturer and to the public.

This information is collected by authority of 15 U.S.C. 2054 and will be entered into a database by a Consumer Product Safety Commission contractor. The information is not retrievable by name. The information may be shared with product manufacturers, distributors, or retailers. However, no names or other personal information will be disclosed without explicit permission.

OMB Control Number 3041-0029

APPENDIX 10:
DEMOGRAPHIC TABLE OF ADULT
TOBACCO USE IN THE UNITED STATES
(1995) (Adults Aged 18 and Older)

DEMOGRAPHIC	PERCENT
All States Overall	23.5
United States Overall	24.7
Men	27.0
Women	22.6
Less than 12 yrs education	30.4
12 yrs education	29.5
More than 12 yrs Education	18.4
Aged 18-24	24.8
Aged 25-44	28.6
Aged 45-64	25.5
Aged 65+	13.0
White	25.6
Black	25.8
Hispanic	18.3
Asian/Pacific Islander	16.6
American Indian/Alaska Native	36.2

Source: United States Department of Health and Human Services Centers for Disease Control and Prevention, National Center for Chronic Disease Prevention and Health Promotion, Office on Smoking and Health.

APPENDIX 11:
SAMPLE TOBACCO PRODUCT LIABILITY COMPLAINT

COMMONWEALTH OF MASSACHUSSETTS, ET. AL, PLAINTIFFS, VS. PHILIP MORRIS, INC., ET. AL., DEFENDANTS.

CIVIL ACTION NUMBER 95-7378 - DECEMBER 19, 1995

COMPLAINT

The Commonwealth of Massachusetts, by Attorney General Scott Harshbarger, for its Complaint alleges as follows:

NATURE OF THE ACTION

1. For years, and continuing to date, the defendant cigarette manufacturers and their trade associations have engaged in a conspiracy to mislead, deceive and confuse the Commonwealth of Massachusetts and its citizens regarding the overwhelming evidence that cigarette smoking causes fatal disease—and that the nicotine in cigarettes is a powerfully addictive substance. Although the cigarette manufacturers promised the Massachusetts public that they would lead the effort to discover and disclose the truth about smoking and health, they have, in fact, systematically suppressed and concealed material information and waged an aggressive campaign of disinformation about the health consequences of cigarette smoking. The cigarette manufacturers have taken these actions, even though they have known for years, based on their own secret research, that their products eventually injure or kill the consumer when used exactly as intended.

2. The cigarette manufacturers have known for decades, on the basis of their own long-concealed research, that nicotine is addictive. At the same time, at least certain defendants have developed sophisticated techniques to manipulate the nicotine delivery of cigarettes so as to create and sustain addiction in smokers. Yet publicly the cigarette manufacturers have denied, and continue to deny, that nicotine is addictive

and that they manipulate the nicotine delivery of cigarettes. In April 1994, each of the Chief Executive Officers of the defendant cigarette manufacturers testified before the Congressional Subcommittee on Health and the Environment that nicotine is not addictive.

3. The cigarette manufacturers are engaged in this course of conduct despite their knowledge that the vast majority of new smokers are children and teenagers Of daily smokers, eighty-two percent start before the age of eighteen. Every day more than 3,000 American teenagers begin smoking

4. Each year, more than 10,000 Massachusetts residents die from smoking the defendant cigarette manufacturers' products. Each year, the Commonwealth must spend millions of dollars to purchase or provide medical and related services for Massachusetts citizens suffering from diseases caused by cigarette smoking. Each year, the defendant cigarette manufacturers reap huge profits from the sale of cigarettes in Massachusetts. Each year, the defendant cigarette manufacturers spend millions of dollars on advertising in Massachusetts which has enormous appeal to young people. Each year, more Massachusetts children and teenagers begin smoking.

5. The Commonwealth seeks both monetary damages and injunctive relief for the conduct alleged in this Complaint. Among other things, the Commonwealth seeks a permanent injunction to require the defendants to disclose their research on smoking, addiction and health, to fund a remedial public education campaign on the health consequences of smoking and to fund smoking cessation programs for nicotine-dependent smokers.

THE PARTIES

6. The Attorney General, Scott Harshbarger, brings this action on behalf of the Commonwealth of Massachusetts and its Division of Medical Assistance (collectively, the "Common-wealth") pursuant to his authority under, inter alia, Massachusetts common law, G.L c. 12, §§ 3, 5 and 10, G.L. c. 118E, § 22 and St. 1994, c. 60, § 276 The Attorney General brings this action to obtain declaratory and equitable relief, damages and restitution The Attorney General seeks to recover the smoking-related costs to the Commonwealth, including, but not limited to, increased expenditures for:

a. Medical assistance provided under Massachusetts' Medicaid program pursuant to G.L. c. 118E. Under the medical assistance program, the Commonwealth pays for medical services provided to program recipients. The Commonwealth pays a substantial share of these costs, with the federal government bearing the remaining costs. In fulfilling its statutory duties, the Commonwealth has expended and will expend substantial sums of money due to the increased costs of providing health care services for smoking-related diseases.

b. Medical assistance provided under the Common Health Program pursuant to G.L. c. 118E, §§ 16, 16A. Under this program, the Commonwealth pays for medical services for disabled adults and children who are not eligible for Medicaid. In fulfilling its statutory duties, the Commonwealth has expended and will expend substantial sums of money due to the increased costs of providing health care services for smoking-related diseases.

THE DEFENDANTS

7. Philip Morris Incorporated ("Philip Morris") is a Virginia corporation with its principal place of business at 120 Park Avenue, New York, New York 10017.

8. R.J. Reynolds Tobacco Company ("RJR") is a New Jersey corporation with its principal place of business at North Main Street, Winston-Salem, North Carolina 27102.

9. Brown & Williamson Tobacco Corporation ("Brown & Williamson") is a Delaware corporation with its principal place of business at 1500 Brown & Williamson Tower, Louisville, Kentucky 40202. On information and belief, the American Tobacco Company ("ATC") was purchased by Brown & Williamson and merged into Brown & Williamson. On information and belief, Brown & Williamson has succeeded to the liabilities of ATC either by operation of law, or as a matter of fact.

10. B.A.T. Industries P.L.C. ("B.A.T. Industries") is a British corporation with its principal place of business at Windsor House, 50 Victoria St., London. Through a succession of intermediary corporations and holding companies, B.A.T. Industries is the sole shareholder of Brown & Williamson. Through Brown & Williamson, B.A.T. Industries has placed cigarettes into the stream of commerce with the expectation that substantial sales of cigarettes would be made in the United States and in Massachusetts. B.A.T. Industries has also conducted, or through its agents, subsidiaries, associated companies, and/or co-conspirators, conducted significant research for Brown & Williamson on the topics of smoking, disease and addiction. On information and belief, Brown & Williamson also sent to England research conducted in the United States on the topics of smoking, disease and addiction in order to remove sensitive and inculpatory documents from United States jurisdiction, and such documents were subject to B.A.T Industries' control.

B.A.T. Industries is a participant in the conspiracy described herein and has caused harm in Massachusetts.

11. Lorillard Tobacco Company ("Lorillard") is a Delaware corporation with its principal place of business at 1 Park Avenue, New York, New York 10016.

12. Liggett Group, Inc. ("Liggett") is a Delaware corporation with its principal place of business at 700 West Main Street, Durham, North Carolina 27702.

13. New England Wholesale Tobacco Co., Inc. is a Massachusetts corporation with its principal and/or usual place of business at 231 New Boston Street, Woburn, Massachusetts 01801 (hereinafter "distributor defendant").

14. Albert H. Notini & Sons, Inc. is a Massachusetts corporation with its principal and/or usual place of business at 225 Aiken Street, Lowell, Massachusetts 01853 (hereinafter "distributor defendant").

15. The Council for Tobacco Research—U.S.A., Inc. ("CTR"), successor in interest to the Tobacco Industry Research Committee ("TIRC"), is a nonprofit corporation organized under the laws of the State of New York with its principal place of business at 900 3rd Avenue, New York, New York 10022.

16. The Tobacco Institute, Inc. ("TI") is a nonprofit corporation organized under the laws of the State of New York with its principal place of business at 1875 I Street N.W., Suite 800, Washington, D.C. 20006.

17. As used in this complaint, the term "defendant" includes all predecessor and successor entities to the named defendants.

18. All defendants did and continue to do business in the Commonwealth; made contracts to be performed in whole or in part in the Commonwealth; and/or manufactured, tested, sold, offered for sale, supplied, or placed in the stream of commerce, or in the course of business, materially participated with others in so doing, cigarettes; and performed such acts as were intended to, and did, result in the sale and distribution in the Commonwealth of cigarettes from which the defendants derived substantial revenue. All defendants also caused tortious injury by acts or omissions in the Commonwealth, and/or caused tortious injury in the Commonwealth by acts or omissions outside the Commonwealth.

JURISDICTION AND VENUE

19. This Court has jurisdiction over the subject matter of this action pursuant to, inter alia, G.L. c. 212, § 4, and G.L. c. 214, §§ 1 and 5. This

Court has personal jurisdiction over the defendants pursuant to G.L. c. 223A, § 3.

20. Venue is proper in Middlesex County pursuant to G.L. c. 223, § 5.

THE HEALTH CONSEQUENCES OF SMOKING

21. The human tragedy of smoking-related disease is practically beyond comprehension. Cigarette smoking is the leading cause of premature death in the United States. According to the federal Centers for Disease Control and Prevention, each year cigarette smoking kills more than 400,000 Americans, exceeding the combined deaths caused by automobile accidents, AIDS, alcohol use, use of illegal drugs, homicide, suicide and fires. Smoking-related illnesses account for one of every five deaths each year in the United States.

22. At least 43 chemicals in the smoke inhaled by persons using defendant cigarette manufacturers' products have been determined to be carcinogenic. Cigarette smoking causes more than 851 of all lung cancer, which has now surpassed breast cancer as the primary cause of death from cancer among women. Smoking is also linked to cancers of the mouth, larynx, esophagus, stomach, pancreas, uterus, cervix, kidney and colon, among others.

23. Smoking is the cause of more than ___ of deaths from pulmonary diseases such as emphysema and bronchitis. These chronic obstructive lung diseases have a profound social impact because of the extended disability of their victims.

24. Cigarette smoking is one of three major independent causes of coronary heart disease. Smoking is also responsible for thousands of deaths from cardiovascular disease, including stroke, heart attack, peripheral vascular disease and aortic aneurysm. Smoking is also linked to a large number of other serious illnesses.

25. The health consequences of smoking among women are of special concern because of the deleterious effect on reproduction. Smoking reduces fertility, increases the rate of miscarriages and stillbirths, retards uterine fetal growth and results in lower birth weights in infants.

26. The nicotine in cigarettes is addictive. Nicotine is recognized as an addictive substance by such major medical organizations as the Office of the U.S. Surgeon General, the World Health Organization, the American Medical Association, the American Psychiatric Association, the American Psychological Association, the American Society of Addiction Medicine, and the Medical Research Council in the United Kingdom. All of these organizations acknowledge tobacco use as a form of drug dependence or addiction with severe adverse health consequences.

1994 CONGRESSIONAL TESTIMONY BY CIGARETTE MANUFACTURERS

27. Last year, the chief executives of the defendant cigarette manufacturers testified under oath before the Subcommittee on Health and the Environment of the Committee on Energy and Commerce, U.S. House of Representatives, chaired by Congressman Waxman ("Waxman Subcommittee"). These executives knowingly made material misrepresentations and/or omissions to the Subcommittee about smoking, health and addiction, and in particular, stated that nicotine is not addictive. These statements were made with the knowledge that they would be communicated to Massachusetts consumers. These defendants' testimony to the Waxman Subcommittee included the following:

a. Andrew Tisch, then CEO of Lorillard, asserted that smoking does not cause cancer. "We have looked at the data and the data that we have been able to see has all been statistical data that has not convinced me that smoking causes death."

b. Philip Morris President and CEO William I. Campbell, said that:

i. "Philip Morris does not manipulate nor independently control the level of nicotine in our products."

ii. "Cigarette smoking is not addictive."

iii. "Philip Morris research does not establish that smoking is addictive."

c. RJR CEO James W. Johnston said that, "smoking is no more 'addictive' than coffee, tea or Twinkies."

28. These representations were made despite a substantial body of evidence, including evidence developed by the cigarette manufacturers themselves, dating from as early as 1962, indicating that nicotine is not only addictive, but is the reason why people smoke.

29. The cigarette manufacturers continue to deny that nicotine is addictive and instead use various misleading euphemisms to describe the role of nicotine, such as "satisfaction," "impact," "strength," "rich aroma" and "pleasure." Nonetheless, there is widespread agreement in the medical and scientific communities that the primary, if not sole, function of nicotine is to provide a pharmacological effect on the smoker that leads to addiction.

THE COMPOSITION OF THE CIGARETTE INDUSTRY IN THE UNITED STATES

30. At all relevant times, Philip Morris, RJR, Brown & Williamson, B.A.T. Industries, Lorillard, Liggett and ATC (hereafter sometimes collectively

"the cigarette manufacturers") together control virtually 100% of the cigarette market in Massachusetts and in the United States.

31. The cigarette industry is one of the most profitable industries in the United States, with profit margins estimated to be in the range of 301. Industry profits are in the billions of dollars annually from domestic sales alone.

32. The unusually small and highly profitable cigarette industry has facilitated the planning, implementation and funding of a decades-long conspiracy by the cigarette manufacturers and their trade associations relating to the issues of smoking, health and addiction.

NATURE OF THE CONSPIRACY

33. This action arises out of an ongoing conspiracy by the leading cigarette manufacturers and their trade associations which together control the cigarette industry in Massachusetts.

34. The cigarette manufacturers have pursued a conspiracy of deceit and misrepresentation against the public designed to protect cigarette sales. The means by which the cigarette manufacturers carried out their conspiracy were twofold: first, they agreed falsely to represent to the public that questions about smoking and health would be answered by a new unbiased and therefore trustworthy source; and second, they counted on that trust to more effectively misrepresent, suppress and confuse the facts about the health dangers of smoking, including addiction. The cigarette manufacturers set their plan in motion by creating a joint industry research organization in 1954. Since that time, they have used the credibility gained by claims of disinterested industry funded research better to misrepresent the material facts to the public. In what has become the industry "mantra," cigarette manufacturers claim that there is insufficient "objective" research to determine if cigarette smoking causes disease, and that cigarettes are not addictive.

35. The two interconnected strategies of misrepresenting their objectivity to gain credibility, and using that credibility better to deceive the public about smoking and health, have been repeated consistently for more than four decades. The cigarette manufacturers and their trade associations have engaged in a continuous conspiracy to deceive the public regarding facts material to the decision to purchase cigarettes.

36. Moreover, as internal industry research confirmed the dangers of smoking and addiction, their deception rose to a new level: they concealed their own negative health and addiction research results from both the public and public health officials. These research results have still not been voluntarily released. But the internal research that has

become available directly contradicts what the cigarette manufacturers and their trade associations have told the public for decades.

37. The cigarette manufacturers have also not told the public that they manipulate and control the nicotine content and delivery of their products to create and sustain smokers' addiction to cigarettes.

38. The success of the industry's campaign of deceit and misinformation depended on the cigarette manufacturers acting in concert. If one company broke ranks and told the public what it knew about the health consequences of cigarette smoking, or its addictive nature, the conspiracy would fail. Without the agreement of each cigarette manufacturer to suppress the truth, the deception that the joint industry research efforts were objective would be revealed, and the substantive claim that "not enough facts are known" to indict cigarette smoking as a cause of disease would ring hollow. The cigarette manufacturers agreed to come together and to stay together in order to accomplish what could not have otherwise occurred—the unified and consistent distortion of public information on smoking, health and addiction.

39. The testimony of the cigarette manufacturers before Congress last year that smoking is not a proven cause of disease and death, and that nicotine is not addictive, is only one recent example of this ongoing pattern of deception and suppression that began more than 40 years ago.

I. CIGARETTE SMOKING AND DISEASE: THE INDUSTRY'S PUBLIC AND PRIVATE RESPONSES

1953 "Big Scare" and the Joint Industry Response

40. In December of 1953, Dr. Ernest L. Wynder of the Sloan Kettering Institute published the results of a study where he painted the shaved backs of mice with cigarette smoke condensate residue. Malignant tumors grew in 44% of the mice in Dr. Wynder's study, providing biological evidence that cigarette smoke caused cancer. The previous year, a British researcher, Dr. Richard Doll, published a statistical analysis showing that lung cancer was more common among people who smoked and that the risk of lung cancer was directly proportional to the number of cigarettes smoked. The widespread reporting of these studies caused what cigarette company officials later called the "Big Scare."

41. The cigarette industry responded quickly to the mounting adverse publicity of a link between smoking and cancer. The Chief Executive Officers of the leading cigarette manufacturers met on December 15, 1953, at the Plaza Hotel in New York City. Also in attendance was the public relations firm of Hill and Knowlton which was to play a central role in formulating and executing the industry response.

42. According to a Hill and Knowlton memorandum summarizing the meeting, cigarette industry executives viewed the problem as "extremely serious and worthy of drastic action." The document continues, "officials stated that salesmen in the industry are frantically alarmed and that the decline in tobacco stocks on the stock exchange market has caused grave concern. . . ."

43. The participants in the meeting agreed that a strong public relations response from the industry was necessary. From the beginning, the emerging research linking smoking and cancer was viewed by these defendants as a public relations problem, not a public health issue. According to the Hill and Knowlton memorandum summarizing the meeting:

> a. The Chief Executive Officers of all the leading companies, except Liggett, "agreed to go along with a public relations program on the health issue."

> b. "They are also emphatic in saying that the entire activity is a long-term, continuing program, since they feel that the problem is one of promoting cigarettes and protecting them from these and other attacks that may be expected in the future."

> c. "The current plans are for Hill and Knowlton to serve as the operating agency of the companies, hiring all the staff and disbursing all funds."

Creation of Tobacco Industry Research Committee

44. Nine days later, Hill and Knowlton presented a detailed recommendation to the cigarette manufacturers and others. The recommendation recognized the importance of gaining the public trust, and avoiding the appearance of bias, if the "pro-cigarette" industry strategy was to be successful According to the memorandum:

> "[T]he grave nature of a number of recently highly publicized research reports on the effects of cigarette smoking. . . have confronted the industry with a serious problem of public relations. It is important that the industry do nothing to appear in the light of being callous to considerations of health or of belittling medical research which goes against cigarettes. The situation is one of extreme delicacy. There is much at stake and the industry group, in moving into the field of public relations, needs to exercise great care not to add fuel to the flames."

45. As a result of the meeting of December 15, 1953, and the recommendations of Hill and Knowlton, five of the six cigarette manufacturers a-treed to create the Tobacco Industry Research Committee ("TIRC"). Liggett joined the industry trade group in 1964, the same year the Sur-

geon General issued his first report linking cigarette smoking to lung cancer. Also in 1964, TIRC changed its name to the Council for Tobacco Research ("CTR"). A second trade group, the Tobacco Institute, was formed by cigarette manufacturers in 1958.

TIRC Control by Hill and Knowlton

46. As had been proposed at the December 15, 1953 meeting, the cigarette manufacturers (except Liggett), through their agent Hill and Knowlton, operated, and effectively controlled TIRC.

47. TIRC was physically established in the Empire State building, one floor below the Hill and Knowlton offices. Internal documents confirm that Hill and Knowlton, and not independent scientists, actually ran TIRC. A "highly confidential" internal memo reported:

> "Since the [TIRC] had no headquarters and no staff, Hill and Knowlton, Inc. was asked to provide a working staff and temporary office space. As a first organizational step, public relations counsel assigned one of its experienced executives, W.T. Hoyt, to serve as account executive and handle as one of his functions the duties of executive secretary for the [TIRC]."

48. In 1954, 35 staff members of Hill and Knowlton worked full or part time for TIRC. In that year, TIRC spent $477,955 on payments to Hill and Knowlton, over 50% of TIRC's entire budget.

The Industry's Promise to Smokers

49. Shortly after creating TIRC, the member cigarette manufacturers made an unambiguous pledge to the public, including the people of Massachusetts and those who advance and protect the public health. These defendants represented that through TIRC, they would conduct and report objective and unbiased research regarding smoking and health. When they made this representation, these defendants knew or should have known that Massachusetts consumers would consider the representation material to their decisions to purchase and smoke cigarettes. At that time, and continuing to the present, these defendants knew or should have known that their failure to fulfill the duty they undertook, and other conduct as alleged herein, would directly increase the health care costs to the Commonwealth.

50. On January 4, 1954, the member defendants announced the formation and purpose of TIRC, with a full page newspaper advertisement entitled "A Frank Statement to Cigarette Smokers." The statement appeared in 448 newspapers across the nation, reaching a circulation of 43,245,000 in 258 cities. The advertisement ran in the daily newspapers in Boston, Springfield and Worcester, Massachusetts.

51. The "Frank Statement to Cigarette Smokers" stated in part:

a. "Recent reports on experiments with mice have given wide publicity to a theory that cigarette smoking is in some way linked with lung cancer in human beings."

b. "Although conducted by doctors of professional standing, these experiments are not regarded as conclusive in the field of cancer research."

c. "[T]here is no proof that cigarette smoking is one of the causes [of lung cancer]."

d. "We accept an interest in people's health as a basic responsibility, paramount to every other consideration in our business."

e. "We believe the products we make are not injurious to health."

f. "We always have and always will cooperate closely with those whose task it is to safeguard the public health."

g. "We are pledging aid and assistance to the research effort into all phases of tobacco use and health."

h. "For this purpose we are establishing a joint industry group consisting initially of the undersigned. This group will be known as TOBACCO INDUSTRY RESEARCH COMMITTEE."

i. "In charge of the research activities of the Committee will be a scientist of unimpeachable integrity and national repute. In addition there will be an Advisory Board of scientists disinterested in the cigarette industry. A group of distinguished men from medicine, science, and education will be invited to serve on this Board. These scientists will advise the Committee on its research activities."

j. "This statement is being issued because we believe the people are entitled to know where we stand on this matter and what we intend to do about it."

52. By the spring of 1955, the self-defense strategy recommended by Hill and Knowlton and implemented by the industry through the "Frank Statement" was largely successful. Hill and Knowlton reported to TIRC:

a. "progress has been made" . . . "The first 'big scare' continues on the wane"

b. "The research program of the [TIRC] has won wide acceptance in the scientific world as a sincere, valuable and scientific effort."

c. "Positive stories are on the ascendancy."

Industry Knowledge that Smoking is Harmful

53. Even before the sponsors of the Frank Statement represented that "there is no proof that cigarette smoking is one of the causes" of lung cancer, an industry researcher had reported the contrary. As early as 1946, Lorillard chemist H.B. Parmele, who later became Vice President of Research and a member of Lorillard's Board of Directors, wrote to his company's manufacturing committee:

> "Certain scientists and medical authorities have claimed for many years that the use of tobacco contributes to cancer development in susceptible people. Just enough evidence has been presented to justify the possibility of such a presumption."

54. In the years following the 1954 "Frank Statement," and continuing to the present, the cigarette companies have repeatedly acted in breach of their assumed duty to report objective facts on smoking and health. As evidence mounted, both through industry research and truly independent studies, that cigarette smoking causes cancer and other diseases, the cigarette manufacturers and their trade associations continued publicly to represent that nothing was proven against smoking. Internal documents show that the truth was very different. The cigarette manufacturers knew and acknowledged internally the veracity of scientific evidence of the health hazards of smoking, and at the same time suppressed such evidence where they could, and attacked it when it did appear.

55. Internal cigarette industry documents reveal, for example:

a. A 1956 memorandum from the Vice President of Philip Morris' Research and Development Department to top executives at the company regarding the advantages of "ventilated cigarettes" stated that: "Decreased carbon monoxide and nicotine are related to decreased harm to the circulatory system as a result of smoking. . . . Decreased irritation is desirable . . . as a partial elimination of a potential cancer hazard."

b. A 1958 memorandum sent to the Vice President of Research at Philip Morris who later became a member of its Board of Directors from a company researcher stated "the evidence . . . is building up that heavy cigarette smoking contributes to lung cancer either alone or in association with physical and physiological factors. . . ."

c. A 1961 document presented to the Philip Morris Research and Development Committee by the company's Vice President of Research and Development included a section entitled "Reduction of Carcinogens in Smoke." The document stated, in part:

"To achieve this objective will require a major research effort, because

– Carcinogens are found in practically every class of compounds in smoke. This fact prohibits complete solution of the problem by eliminating one or two classes of compounds. The best we can hope for is to reduce a particularly bad class, i.e., the polynuclear hydrocarbons, or phenols. . . .

– Flavor substances and carcinogenic substances come from the same classes, in many instances."

d. A 1963 memorandum to Philip Morris' President and CEO from the company's Vice President of Research describes a number of classes of compounds in cigarette smoke which are "known carcinogens." The document goes on to describe the link between smoking and bronchitis and emphysema. "Irritation problems are now receiving greater attention because of the general medical belief that irritation leads to chronic bronchitis and emphysema. These are serious diseases involving millions of people. Emphysema is often fatal either directly or through other respiratory complications. A number of experts have predicted that the cigarette industry ultimately may be in greater trouble in this area than in the lung cancer field."

e. Brown & Williamson and its parent company, BATCO, researched the health effects of nicotine and were aware early on, as reported at a B.A.T. Group Research Conference in November 1970, that "nicotine may be implicated in the aetiology [cause] of cardiovascular disease. . . ."

f. A 1961 "Confidential" memo-randum from the consulting research firm hired by Liggett to do research for the company states:

"There are biologically active materials present in cigarette tobacco. These are: a) cancer causing; b) cancer promoting; c) poisonous; d) stimulating, pleasurable, and flavorful."

g. A 1963 memorandum from the Liggett consulting research firm states: "Basically, we accept the inference of a causal relationship between the chemical properties of ingested tobacco smoke and the development of carcinoma, which is suggested by the statistical association shown in the studies of Doll and Hill, Horn, and Dorn with some reservations and qualifications and even estimate by how much the incidence of cancer may possibly be reduced if the carcinogenic matter can be diminished, by an appropriate filter, by a given percentage."

56. These internal Liggett documents sharply contrast with the information Liggett provided to the Surgeon General in 1963. Liggett withheld from the Surgeon General the views of its researchers and consultants that the evidence showed cigarette smoking causes human disease.

57. The report Liggett presented to the Surgeon General omitted all of these views. Instead, it focused on alternative causes of disease, such as air pollution, coffee and alcohol consumption, diet, lack of exercise, and genetics. Liggett criticized the known statistical association between smoking and mortality and various diseases as "unreliably conducted" and "inadequately analyzed." The Liggett report concluded that the association between smoking and disease was inconclusive, and was in fact due to other factors coincidentally associated with smoking.

58. Philip Morris also concealed from the public its actual views of the research conducted outside the influence of the industry. In a 1971 memorandum, Dr. H. Wakeham, then Vice President of Research and Development, referring to a recent study which found cigarette smoke inhalation caused lung cancer in beagles: "1970 might very properly be called the year of the beagle. Early in the year, the American Cancer Society announced that they had finally demonstrated the formation of lung cancer in beagles by smoke inhalation in the now infamous Auerbach and Hammond study." Although Dr. Wakeham criticized the mice cancer studies, he conceded that "the beagle test was a critical one . . . for the cigarette causation hypothesis."

59. Dr. Wakeham's memorandum demonstrates Philip Morris' approval of the industry's public dismissals of these independent studies: "The strong opposition of the industry to the beagle test is indicative of a new, more aggressive stance on the part of the industry in the smoking and health controversy. We have gone over from what I have called the 'vigorous denial' approach, the take it on the chin and keep quiet attitude, to the strongly voiced opposition and criticism. I personally think this counter-propaganda is a better stance than the former one."

60. Similarly, BATCO's internal view of the validity of mouse skin painting experiments differed markedly from the view expressed in public statements. Minutes from a 1969 BATCO research conference stated "[h]istorically, bioassay experiments were undertaken by the industry with the object of clarifying the role of smoke constituents in pulmonary carcinogenesis. The most widely used of these methods [was] mouse-skin painting. . . . (a) In the foreseeable future, say five years, mouse-skin painting would remain as the ultimate court of appeal on carcinogenic effects." Two years later a Brown & Williamson public re-

lations document stated that "[m]uch of the experimental work involves mouse-painting or animal smoke inhalation experiments. . . . [T]he results obtained on the skin of mice should not be extrapolated to the lung tissue of the mouse, or to any other animal species. Certainly such skin results should not be extrapolated to the human lung."

Repeated False Promises to the Public

61. The deceptions of the 1954 "Frank Statement to Cigarette Smokers" were renewed and repeated by the industry. RJR chairman Bowman Gray told Congress in 1964: "If it is proven that cigarettes are harmful, we want to do something about it regardless of what somebody else tells us to do. And we would do our level best. It's only human."

62. Another advertisement co-sponsored by TIRC and the Tobacco Institute called "A Statement about Tobacco and Health," stated:

"We recognize that we have a special responsibility to the public—to help scientists determine the facts about tobacco and health, and about certain diseases that have been associated with tobacco use. We accepted this responsibility in 1954 by establishing the TIRC, which provides research grants to independent scientists. We pledge continued support of this program of research until the facts are known." "We shall continue all possible efforts to bring the facts to light."

63. Additional representations were made in 1970 when the cigarette industry through its lobbying group, the Tobacco Institute, placed a number of advertisements similar to the 1954 "Frank Statement." One advertisement stated in part:

a. "After millions of dollars and over 20 years of research: The question about smoking and health is still a question."

b. "In the interest of absolute objectivity, the tobacco industry has supported totally independent research efforts with completely non-restrictive funding."

c. "In 1954, the Industry established what is now known as CTR, the Council for Tobacco Research—USA, to provide financial support for research by independent scientists into all phases of tobacco use and health. Completely autonomous, CTR's research activity is directed by a board of ten scientists and physicians who retain their affiliations with their respective universities and institutions. This board has full authority and responsibility for policy, development and direction of the research effort."

d. "The findings are not secret."

64. Another advertisement in 1970 stated that the industry "believes the American public is entitled to complete, authenticated information about cigarette smoking and health. . . . The tobacco industry recognizes and accepts a responsibility to promote the progress of independent scientific research in the field of tobacco and health."

65. In 1972 Tobacco Institute President Horace Kornegay testifying before Congress, stated that "the cigarette industry is as vitally concerned or more so than any other group in determining whether cigarette smoking causes human disease. . . . That is why the entire tobacco industry . . . since 1954 has committed a total of $40 million for smoking and health research through grants to independent scientists and institutions."

66. In March of 1983, Sheldon Sommers, MD, scientific director of CTR, testified before Congress that: "Cigarette smoking has not been scientifically established to be a cause of chronic diseases, such as cancer, cardiovascular disease, or emphysema. Nor has it been shown to affect pregnancy outcome adversely."

67. In 1984, RJR placed an editorial style advertisement in the "New York Times" stating that "[s]tudies which conclude that smoking causes disease have regularly ignored significant evidence to the contrary."

68. In April 1994, William Campbell, President of Philip Morris, told the Waxman Subcommittee, in response to what he described as "a number of charges . . . leveled against the tobacco industry generally, and Philip Morris specifically. . . :" ". . .our consumers are being misled and when that happens Philip Morris has and will continue to speak out loudly and clearly. Our consumers deserve to know the truth. . . .."

69. Each of the representations by defendants to the public about sponsoring independent objective research and bringing the truth to light were false and deceptive. These misrepresentations seek to gain the trust of the public in order to better distort and suppress substantive information about smoking and health.

The Gentlemen's Agreement

70. This industry strategy depended for its success on joint and concerted action by the cigarette manufacturers and their trade associations. Upon information and belief, each of these defendants agreed not to reveal to the public the true nature of TIRC, and later CTR, and not to disclose adverse information on smoking and health, in order to protect continued cigarette sales.

71. In 1968, a memo addressed to the CEO of Liggett regarding a meeting of the research directors of the six cigarette manufacturers stated on the topic of smoking and health "a general feeling that an industry approach as opposed to an individual company approach was highly desirable."

72. Each company also agreed not to perform research on smoking and health on their own. This agreement was referred to as the "Gentlemen's Agreement." A 1968 internal Philip Morris draft memorandum entitled "Need for biological research by Philip Morris research and development," and prepared by the company's Vice President of Research and Development, states:

> "We have reason to believe that in spite of the gentlemans [sic] agreement for the tobacco industry in previous years that at least some of the major companies have been increasing biological studies with their own facilities."

73. As indicated by the 1968 "Gentlemans Agreement" memo, it was believed within the industry that individual companies were performing certain research on their own, in addition to the joint industry research. But the fundamental understanding and agreement remained intact: that harmful information and activities would be restrained, suppressed, and/or concealed. This included restraining, suppressing, and concealing research on the health effects of smoking, including the addictive qualities of cigarettes, and restraining, concealing, and suppressing the research and marketing of safer cigarettes.

Suppression and Concealment of Industry-Sponsored Biological Research Role of CTR as a "Front"

74. Internal documents demonstrate that the joint industry research efforts undertaken through TIRC, and later, through CTR, were not disinterested or objective. Rather, they were designed and used to promote favorable research, to suppress negative research where possible, and to attack negative research where it could not be suppressed, all in order to convince the public that the "case against smoking is not closed."

75. A 1974 report to the CEO of Lorillard from a research executive described CTR's scientific projects as "hav[ing] not been selected against specific scientific goals, but rather for various purposes such as public relations, political relations, position for litigation, etc. Thus, it seems obvious that reviews of such programs for scientific relevance and merit in the smoking and health field are not likely to produce high ratings."

76. A 1972 internal document from a Tobacco Institute official to the group's President described the importance of using joint industry research to maintain public doubt about the link between smoking and disease: "For nearly twenty years, this industry has employed a single strategy to defend itself on three major fronts—litigation, politics, and public opinion. While the strategy was brilliantly conceived and executed over the years helping us win important battles, it is only fair to say that it is not—nor was it ever intended to be—a vehicle for victory. On the contrary, it has always been a holding strategy, consisting of

- creating doubt about the health charge without actually denying it

- advocating the public's right to smoke, without actually urging them to take up the practice

- encouraging objective scientific research as the only way to resolve the question of the health hazard. "As an industry, therefore, we are committed to an ill-defined middle ground which is articulated by variations on the theme that, 'the case is not proved.'" "In the cigarette controversy, the public—especially those who are present and potential supporters (e.g. tobacco state congressmen and heavy smokers)—must perceive, understand, and believe in evidence to sustain their opinions that smoking may not be the causal factor." "As things stand, we supply them with too little in the way of ready-made credible alternatives."

77. A 1978 memo addressed to the CTR file from a Philip Morris official characterized CTR as "an industry 'shield'." The memorandum goes on to state:

"the 'public relations' value of CTR must be considered and continued. . . . It is extremely important that the industry continue to spend their dollars on research to show that we don't agree that the case against smoking is closed. . . . There is a 'CTR basket' which must be maintained for 'PR' purposes. . . ."

78. In 1993, a former 24-year employee of CTR confirmed publicly that the joint industry research efforts were not objective:

"When CTR researchers found out that cigarettes were bad and it was better not to smoke, we didn't publicize that." "The CTR is just a lobbying thing. We were lobbying for cigarettes."

79. This and other evidence demon-strates that the role and purpose of TIRC and CTR in the cigarette manufacturers' strategy was to seek to use the public's trust to propagate "procigarette" propaganda. An industry official wrote in his personal notes describing a meeting which included high level officials from various cigarette manufacturers that:

"CTR is best & cheapest insurance the tobacco industry can buy and without it the Industry would have to invent CTR or would be dead."

80. Nonetheless, in its annual reports published between 1985 and 1992, CTR stated that its Scientific Advisory Board funded peer-reviewed research projects "judging them solely on the basis of scientific merit and relevance." In 1994, Dr. James F. Glenn, CEO of CTR, submitted testimony to the Waxman Subcommittee that:

a. "[t]he Council . . . sponsors re-search into questions of tobacco use and health and makes the results available to the public."

b. "Council grantees are assured complete scientific freedom in conducting their studies. . . . Publication of research results is encouraged in all instances."

The Example of Dr. Homburger

81. In fact, CTR-sponsored research projects were directed away from research that might add to the evidence against smoking. When CTR-sponsored research did produce unfavorable results, however, the information was distorted or simply suppressed For example, Dr. Freddy Homburger, a researcher in Cambridge, Massachusetts, undertook a study of smoke exposure on hamsters. According to Dr. Homburger, he received a grant from CTR which was changed half-way through the study to a contract "so they could control publication—they were quite open about that." Dr. Homburger has testified that when the study was completed in 1974, the Scientific Director of CTR and a CTR lawyer "didn't want us to call anything cancer" and that they threatened Dr. Homburger with "never get[ting] a penny more" if his paper was published without deleting the word cancer.

82. An internal CTR document describes how Dr. Homburger attempted to call a press conference about the incident and how CTR stopped it:

"He. . . was to tell the press that the tobacco industry was attempting to suppress important scientific informa-tion about the harmful effects of smoking. He was going to point specifically at CTR." "I arranged later that evening for it to be canceled." "Homburger was given a cordial welcome and nicely hastened" [sic] out the door." "P.S. I doubt if you or Tom will want to retain this note."

CTR Special Products Division

83. Another mechanism that CTR used to suppress research results that implicated smoking in disease was selectively to involve lawyers, and then invoke the attorney/client privilege to prevent the disclosure of harmful information. CTR used the term "special projects" to mean a project that carried a risk of a negative result that might have to be sup-

pressed. "Special projects" were selected and monitored by industry lawyers to prevent disclosure. One Philip Morris official characterized CTR as a "front" for performing "special projects."

84. Notes prepared at a 1981 meeting of the cigarette industry's Committee of General Counsel state:

> "When we started the CTR Special Projects, the idea was that the scientific director of CTR would review a project. If he liked it, it was a CTR special project. If he did not like it, then it became a lawyers' special project." ". . . we were afraid of discovery for FTC and Aviado, we wanted to protect it under the lawyers. We did not want it out in the open."

85. At least one cigarette company used similar tactics to suppress and avoid disclosure of its internal research on smoking and disease. At a time when the company was resisting discovery in a number of personal injury lawsuits, Brown & Williamson's general counsel, J. Kendrick Wells, recommended in a memorandum dated January 17, 1985, that much of the company's biological research be declared "deadwood" and shipped to England. He recommended that no notes, memos or lists be made about these documents. Wells stated, "I had marked certain of the document references with an X. . . which I suggested were deadwood in the behavioral and biological studies area. I said that the "B" series are "Janus" series studies and should also be considered as deadwood." ("Janus" was a name of a project that attempted to isolate and remove the harmful elements of tobacco.) Wells further recommended that the research, development and engineering department also should undertake "to remove the deadwood from the files."

86. Through CTR, the cigarette manufacturers have used lawyers and the claim of attorney/client privilege to insulate CTR-funded research projects from disclosure to the public and to government officials. This conduct demonstrates the falsity of the industry representations jointly to fund objective research, and to report the results of that research to the public.

Suppression and Concealment of Internal Biological Research Mouse House Massacre

87. In the 1960s, RJR established a facility in Winston/Salem, North Carolina, to perform research on the health effects of smoking using mice Nicknamed the "Mouse House," RJR scientists conducted research in a number of specific areas, including studies of the actual mechanism whereby smoking causes emphysema in the lungs.

88. The RJR lab made significant progress in understanding this mechanism. Despite this progress, RJR disbanded the entire research division in one day, and fired all 26 scientists without notice.

89. Several months before the 1970 closure and firings, RJR attorneys collected dozens of research notebooks from the scientists. The notebooks have still not been disclosed. One of the researchers later stated about RJR's executives and lawyers that "they like to take the position that you can't prove harm because you don't know mechanism. . . . And sitting right under their noses is evidence of mechanism[.] What are they going to do with this stuff? They decided to kill it."

90. Internally, an RJR-commissioned report favorably described the Mouse House work as "the more important of the smoking and health research effort because it comes close to determining what was thought to be the underlying pathobiology of emphysema." None of the work done at the "Mouse House" was disclosed to the public.

Safer Cigarette

91. Several cigarette manufacturers' biological research appears to have been directed toward developing a cigarette with reduced health risks. These companies performed research which involved dividing cigarette smoke into its different chemical constituents, or "fractions." to discover which part of the cigarette smoke caused disease. Several companies were successful in discovering which specific constituents in tobacco smoke were carcinogens, or were linked to other diseases. This research was kept secret and never reported to the public.

92. number of companies also successfully removed certain harmful constituents from cigarette smoke, and developed prototype cigarettes with reduced health effects. These products were never marketed.

93. A memorandum written by an attorney at the firm of Shook, Hardy & Bacon, long-time lawyers for the cigarette industry, articulated the industry-wide position regarding the issue of a safer cigarette. The 1987 memorandum, referring to the marketing by RJR of a smokeless cigarette, Premier, stated that the smokeless cigarette could "have significant effects on the tobacco industry's joint defense efforts" and that "[t]he industry position has always been that there is no alternative design for a cigarette as we know them." The attorney also noted that, "Unfortunately, the Reynolds announcement... seriously undercuts this component of industry's defense."

94. As early as 1958, a memorandum from a Philip Morris researcher to the company's Vice President of Research and Development proposed that the company attempt to make a safer cigarette that could enable it

to "jump on the other side of the fence. . . on the issue of tobacco smoking and health. . ."

95. Philip Morris did perform the research and development of such a product. However, the company never released the research, and never informed the public that existing cigarettes were not safe or that a safer cigarette was possible. A 1964 Philip Morris research and development presentation to its Board of Directors stated:

> "Two years ago, in anticipation of a health crisis to be precipitated by the Smoking and Health Report of the Surgeon General's Committee, we undertook to develop a physiologically superior cigarette.

> [W]e put together a charcoal filter product with performance superior to anything in the market place. That product was known as Saratoga. Physiologically it was an outstanding cigarette. Unfortunately then after much discussion we decided not to tell the physiological story which might have appealed to a health conscious segment of the market. The product as test marketed didn't have good 'taste' and consequently was unacceptable to the public ignorant of its physiological superiority."

96. The research and development department at Philip Morris nonetheless viewed continued research into safer cigarettes as necessary to compete in the event that another cigarette company marketed a safer cigarette. The presentation to the Philip Morris Board of Directors continued: "The Research and Development Department is working to establish a strong technological base with both defensive and offensive capabilities in the smoking and health situation. Our philosophy is not to start a war, but if war comes, we aim to fight well and to win."

Liggett Safer Cigarette: XA

97. Liggett also developed a safer cigarette. Company researchers believed that they had discovered which cigarette smoke constituents were carcinogens, and found a way to remove them. Despite Liggett officials' belief that the product was commercially marketable, the company never marketed the safer cigarette and suppressed the research that led to its development.

98. Liggett began its research by repeating the smoke condensate painting studies of mice performed by Dr. Wynder through a contract with a consulting firm. The consulting firm confirmed Dr. Wynder's findings, and as a result in 1968, Liggett began "a tobacco additive program designed to reduce or eliminate the tumorigenic activity of cigarette smoke."

99. By 1979, Liggett had declared the work a success. Company documents state:

"Briefly, as a result of 20 years effort in cooperation with [the consulting firm], we have developed a cigarette system which produces smoke of reduced biological activity. . . . [T]here can be no argument that the use of the additives has resulted in a product with lower carcinogenic effects. . . .."

100. Liggett's safer cigarette, a product called "XA," was never marketed and the XA project was abandoned. On information and belief, Liggett did so for two reasons. First, disclosing the feasibility of a safer cigarette would imply that all existing cigarettes were not safe. Second, Philip Morris apparently threatened Liggett with retaliation if Liggett violated the industry agreement not to disclose negative information on smoking and health. Liggett's Assistant Research Director, Dr. James Mold, reported that Liggett's president said that he was "told by someone in the Philip Morris Company that if we tried to market such a product that they would clobber us."

Liggett, James Mold and the Suppression of the XA Research

101. During the XA project, Liggett attempted to insulate the research by the use of company lawyers. According to Dr. Mold, after 1975, "all meetings that we had regarding this project were to be attended by a lawyer. . . . All paper that was generated. . . [was] to be directed to the Law Department." Dr. Mold stated that lawyers even collected all the notes after each meeting.

102. Dr. Mold stated that despite its significance, the company lawyers not only ultimately succeeded in stopping the project, but ordered him not to publish the results of the research that led to the safer cigarette. Only an abstract of the paper, modified by the legal department, was published by the consulting firm, without Dr. Mold's name.

103. When asked why Liggett never marketed the safer XA cigarette, Dr. Mold explained that:

"[Management circles] felt that such a cigarette if put on the market would seriously indict them for having sold other types of cigarettes that didn't contain this, for example. Or that they were carrying on this biological research at the same time saying it meant nothing."

Liggett Safer Cigarette Patent

104. Liggett had also obtained a patent for the process it had discovered to produce its safer cigarette. The patent application described the reduction in cancer in mouse studies, prompting stories in the media that Liggett was the first cigarette company to admit that smoking caused

cancer. Liggett responded by issuing a press release it called a "Liggettgram" which stated:

> "Liggett and the cigarette industry continue to deny, as they have consistently, that any conclusions can be drawn relating such test results on mice in laboratories to cancer in human beings. It has never been established that smoking is a cause of human cancer." "The laboratory experiments reported in the patent were conducted for Liggett by an independent researcher, The Life Sciences Division of Arthur D. Little, Inc."

105. At the time Liggett made this statement, Dr. Mold estimates that Liggett had spent a total of $10 million on research involving mice, in part to develop the safer XA cigarette. Liggett's internal reports on the benefit of the XA, and the absence of increased risk of harm from the additives used, specifically used animal studies as reliable indicators of the health effect of the product on humans.

106. Despite overwhelming scientific evidence, and the confirmation of this evidence by their own internal research, the cigarette manufacturers and their trade associations continue to this day to repeat over and over, in a unified stance, that there is no causal connection between cigarette smoking and adverse health effects. These representations are misleading, deceptive and untrue. They rest at the heart of the industry's ongoing conspiracy to market and profit from a product it knows is deadly.

II. THE ROLE OF NICOTINE IN SMOKING

107. The other fact that the cigarette industry has made every effort to conceal and deny is that nicotine is a powerfully addictive substance. While carefully studying its addictive character and acting upon that knowledge to maintain cigarette sales, each of the cigarette manufacturers has denied that nicotine is addictive.

108. This public deception and the industry's secret manipulation of nicotine were and are critically important to the cigarette manufacturers. As objective researchers increased their warnings of the health dangers of cigarettes, nicotine addiction kept people smoking. This second front in their strategy to sell their dangerous products allows the cigarette manufacturers to continue to sell their dangerous products -even to those who eventually come to doubt the industry's health claims. And if a new consumer is fooled for a time by "procigarette" disinformation on health, and takes up the habit, it may well be too late. Instead of a simple decision not to purchase a product, the consumer must fight an addiction.

Industry Knowledge of the Addictiveness of Nicotine

109. Cigarette manufacturers have known since at least the early 1960s, of the addictive properties of the nicotine contained in the cigarettes they manufacture and sell. Industry documents are replete with evidence of such knowledge:

a. In 1962, Sir Charles Ellis, scientific advisor to the board of directors of British American Tobacco Company ("BATCO"), Brown & Williamson's parent company, stated at a meeting of BATCO's worldwide subsidiaries, that "smoking is a habit of addiction" and that "[n]icotine is not only a very fine drug, but the technique of administration by smoking has considerable psychological advan-tages. . .." He subsequently described Brown & Williamson as being "in the nicotine rather than the tobacco industry."

b. A research report from 1963 commissioned by Brown & Williamson states that when a chronic smoker is denied nicotine: "A body left in this unbalanced state craves for renewed drug intake in order to restore the physiological equilibrium. This uncon-scious desire explains the addiction of the individual to nicotine." No information from that research has ever been voluntarily disclosed to the public.

c. Addison Yeaman, general counsel at Brown & Williamson, summarized his view about nicotine in an internal memorandum also in 1963: "Moreover, nicotine is addictive. We are, then, in the business of selling nicotine, an addictive drug effective in the release of stress mechanisms."

d. Internal reports prepared by Philip Morris in 1972 and the Philip Morris U.S.A. Research Center in March 1978, demonstrate Philip Morris' understanding of the role of nicotine in tobacco use: "We think that most smokers can be considered nicotine seekers, for the pharmacological effect of nicotine is one of the rewards that come from smoking. When the smoker quits, he foregoes [sic] his accustomed nicotine. The change is very noticeable, he misses the reward, and so he returns to smoking."

e. From 1940-1970, ATC conducted its own nicotine research, funding over 90 studies on the pharmacological and other effects of nicotine on the body, 80% of all biological studies funded by ATC over this period. In 1969, ATC even test marketed a nicotine-enriched cigarette in Seattle, Washington.

f. In a 1972 document entitled "RJR confidential research planning memorandum on the nature of the tobacco business and the crucial role of nicotine therein," an RJR executive wrote: "In a sense, the tobacco industry may be thought of as being a specialized, highly ritualized, and stylized segment of the pharmaceutical industry. Tobacco products uniquely contain and deliver nicotine, a potent drug with a variety of physiological effects."

Suppression and Concealment of Research on Nicotine Addiction

110. The cigarette manufacturers, rather than fulfilling their promise to the public to disclose material information about smoking and health, chose a course of suppression, concealment, and disinformation about the true properties of nicotine and the addictiveness of smoking.

111. Philip Morris hired Victor DeNoble in 1980 to study nicotine's effects on the behavior of rats and to research and test potential nicotine analogues. DeNoble, in turn, recruited Paul C. Mele, a behavioral pharmacologist.

112. DeNoble and Mele discovered that nicotine met two of the hallmarks of potential addiction—self-administration (rats would press levers to inject themselves with a nicotine solution) and tolerance (a given dose of nicotine over time had a reduced effect).

113. However, Philip Morris instructed DeNoble and Mele to keep their work secret, even from fellow Philip Morris scientists. Test animals were delivered at dawn and brought from the loading dock to the laboratory under cover.

114. DeNoble was later told by lawyers for the company that the data he and Mele were generating could be dangerous Philip Morris executives began talking of killing the research or moving it outside of the company so Philip Morris would have more freedom to disavow the results.

115. In August 1983, Philip Morris ordered DeNoble to withdraw from publication a research paper on nicotine that had already been accepted for publication after full peer review by the journal Psychopharmacology. According to DeNoble, the company changed its mind because it did not want its own research showing nicotine was addictive or harmful to compromise the company's defense in litigation recently filed against it. He said that Philip Morris officials had rightly interpreted the suppressed nicotine studies as showing that, in terms of addictiveness, "nicotine looked like heroin."

116. In April 1984, Philip Morris closed DeNoble's nicotine research lab. DeNoble and Mele were forced abruptly to halt their studies, turn off all their instruments and turn in their security badges by morning. Philip Morris executives threatened them with legal action if they published or talked about their nicotine research. According to DeNoble, the lab liter-

ally vanished overnight. The animals were killed, the equipment was removed and all traces of the former lab were eliminated.

117. DeNoble testified to the Waxman Subcommittee that "senior research management in Richmond, Va., as well as top officials at the Philip Morris Company in New York, continually reviewed our research and approved our research." DeNoble also stated that these officials were specifically told that nicotine was a drug of abuse.

118. Brown & Williamson undertook its potentially sensitive research on nicotine through a contractor in Geneva, Switzerland, and through British affiliates at an English lab called Harrogate.

119. In 1963, Brown & Williamson debated internally whether to disclose to the U.S. Surgeon General, who was preparing his first official report on smoking and health, what the company knew about the addictiveness of nicotine and the adverse effects of smoking on health. Addison Yeaman, general counsel, advised Brown & Williamson to "accept its responsibility" and disclose its findings to the Surgeon General. He said that such disclosure would then allow the company openly to research and develop a safer cigarette.

120. Brown & Williamson rejected Yeaman's advice to make full disclosure to the Surgeon General. A series of six letters and telexes exchanged by Yeaman and senior BATCO official A.D. McCormick between June 28 and August 8, 1963, document the company's decision not to disclose its research findings to the Surgeon General. That research, some of which was later characterized in a report in the Journal of the American Medical Association as "at the cutting edge of nicotine pharmacology," preceded the main published reports from the general scientific community by several years.

The Industry's Interest in Nicotine

121. A chronology of the industry's research and development activities confirms that the cigarette manufacturers understood early on that nicotine was the key to their industry's success. The industry has conducted extensive research establishing that smokers require a certain level of nicotine from their cigarettes and that tobacco "satisfaction" is attributable to nicotine's effect on the body after absorption.

122. Philip Morris internal reports from 1972 and 1978 characterize the role of nicotine in tobacco use: "The cigarette should be conceived not as a product but as a package. The product is nicotine. . . . Think of the cigarette pack as a storage container for a day's supply of nicotine. . . . Think of the cigarette as a dispenser for a dose unit of nicotine."

123. Documents from a BATCO study called Project Hippo, uncovered only in May 1994, show that as far back as 1961, this cigarette company was actively studying the physiological and pharmacological effects of nicotine. Project Hippo reports were circulated to other U.S. cigarette manufacturers and to TIRC, demonstrating that at least some of the industry's nicotine research was shared. BATCO sent the reports to officials at Brown & Williamson and RJR, and circulated a copy to TIRC with a request that TIRC "consider whether it would help the U.S industry for these reports to be passed on to the Surgeon General's Committee."

124. Similarly, an RJR-MacDonald Marketing Summary Report from 1983 concluded that the primary reason people smoke "is probably the physiological satisfaction provided by the nicotine level of the product."

125. To this day, the cigarette manufacturers have concealed from the public and public health officials their extensive knowledge of the addictive properties of nicotine and its critical role in smoking.

126. As recently as December 1995, the Wall Street Journal reported on an internal Philip Morris draft document analyzing the competitive market for nicotine products for the years 1990 - 1992. The report describes the importance of nicotine:

> "Different people smoke for different reasons. But the primary reason 1S CO deliver nicotine into their bodies. . . . It is a physiologically active, nitrogen containing substance. Similar organic chemicals include nicotine, quinine, cocaine, atropine and morphine. While each of these substances can be used to affect human physiology, nicotine has a particularly broad range of influence. During the smoking act, nicotine is inhaled into the lungs in smoke, enters the bloodstream and travels to the brain in about eight to ten seconds."

127. The cigarette manufacturers have long understood that reducing or eliminating nicotine from their products would hurt sales. As one company researcher wrote in a 1978 report to Philip Morris executives:

> "If the industry's introduction of acceptable low-nicotine products does make it easier for dedicated smokers to quit, then the wisdom of the introduction is open to debate."

128. Instead, the industry attempted to develop ostensibly safer ways of delivering adequate doses of nicotine to create and sustain addiction in the smoker.

129. Some members of the industry studied artificial nicotine or nicotine analogues that would have the addictive and psychopharmacological properties of nicotine without its dangerous effects on the heart. Dr.

DeNoble was hired by Philip Morris, in part, to research and develop a nicotine analogue.

130. DeNoble did discover such an analogue, but Philip Morris chose to halt its effort to determine whether the nicotine analogue could be used to make a safer cigarette. On information and belief, Philip Morris decided not to pursue nicotine analogues in order to avoid the risk of adverse publicity and of compromising the industry's consistent position that there was no alternative design for cigarettes.

131. Brown & Williamson also understood that nicotine was the essential ingredient in maintaining tobacco sales. The company attempted to develop a "safer" cigarette which internal documents described as "a nicotine delivery device."

132. By the end of the 1970's, however, Brown & Williamson, in a pattern that was repeated throughout the industry, closed its research labs and halted all work on a safer cigarette.

133. RJR's efforts to develop a safer cigarette also focused on delivering nicotine to the consumer without the harmful constituents of tobacco smoke. In the late 1980's, RJR developed and test marketed Premier, a smokeless and virtually tobacco-free cigarette which was, in essence, a nicotine delivery system.

134. The cigarette manufacturers have affirmatively misrepresented to consumers and to Congress the role of nicotine in tobacco use. Even today, Brown & Williamson, RJR and TI continue to claim that nicotine is important in cigarettes for taste and "mouth-feel." However, tobacco industry patents specifically distinguish nicotine from flavorants and an RJR book on flavoring tobacco, while listing approximately a thousand flavorants, fails to include nicotine as a flavoring agent. The cigarette industry has actually concentrated on developing technologies to mask the acrid flavor of increased levels of nicotine in cigarettes.

Industry Control and Manipulation of Nicotine

135. Cigarette manufacturers have developed and used highly sophisticated technologies designed to deliver nicotine in precisely calculated quantities—quantities that are more than sufficient to create and sustain addiction in the vast majority of individuals who smoke regularly. Cigarette manufacturers control the nicotine content of their products through selective breeding and cultivation of plants for nicotine content, and careful tobacco leaf purchasing plans. The companies control nicotine delivery (i.e. the amount received by the smoker) with various design and manufacturing techniques.

Manipulation of Nicotine Content: Y-1

136. The story of Brown & Williamson's development of a new tobacco plant dubbed "Y-1" is one of the more egregious examples of the cigarette industry's concealment of its control and manipulation of the nicotine levels in its products.

137. On June 21, 1994, Dr. David A. Kessler told the Waxman Subcommittee that FDA investigators had discovered that Brown & Williamson had developed a high nicotine tobacco plant, which the company called "Y-1." This discovery followed Brown & Williamson's flat denial to the FDA on May 3, 1994, that it had engaged in "any breeding of tobacco for high or low nicotine levels."

138. When four FDA investigators visited the Brown & Williamson plant in Macon, Georgia on May 3, 1994, Brown & Williamson officials denied that the company was involved in breeding tobacco for specific nicotine levels. Only after the FDA had learned of the development of Y-1 in its investigation and confronted company officials with the evidence did the company admit that it was growing and using the high-nicotine plant.

139. In fact, in a decade-long project, Brown & Williamson secretly developed a genetically-engineered tobacco plant with a nicotine content more than twice the average found naturally in flue-cured tobacco. Brown & Williamson took out a Brazilian patent for the new plant, which was printed in Portuguese. Brown & Williamson and a Brazilian sister company, Souza Cruz Overseas, grew Y-1 in Brazil and shipped it to the United States where it was used in five Brown & Williamson cigarette brands sold in Massachusetts. including three labeled "light." When the company's deception was uncovered, company officials admitted that close to four million pounds of Y-1 were stored in company warehouses in the United States.

140. As part of its cover-up, Brown & Williamson even went so far as to instruct the DNA Plant Technology Corporation of Oakland, California, which had developed Y-1, to tell FDA investigators that Y-1 had "never [been] commercialized." Only after the FDA discovered two United States Customs Service invoices indicating that "more than a half-million pounds" of Y-1 tobacco had been shipped to Brown & Williamson on September 21, 1992, did the company admit that it had developed the high-nicotine tobacco.

141. Y-1 is one example of an overall trend in the tobacco industry to increase the nicotine content of tobaccos. American tobaccos of all types have undergone cumulative increases in total nicotine levels since the 1950s. Nicotine levels in the most widely grown American tobaccos in-

creased between 10-50 percent between 1955 and 1980. On information and belief, this increase is the result of the industry's active and controlling participation in efforts to breed and cultivate tobacco for high nicotine levels.

Manipulation of Nicotine Delivery

142. The nicotine content of the raw tobacco is not the only variable manipulated by the cigarette manufacturers to deliver a pharmacologically active dose of nicotine to the smoker. Cigarettes are nor simply cut tobacco rolled into a paper tube. Modern cigarettes as sold in Massachusetts are painstakingly designed and manufactured to control nicotine delivery to the smoker.

143. For example, cigarette manufac-turers add several ammonia compounds during the manufacturing process which increase the delivery of nicotine and almost double the nicotine transfer efficiency of cigarettes.

144. Just this year, Brown & Williamson publicly denied that the use of ammonia in the processing of tobacco increases the amount of nicotine absorbed by the smoker. Nevertheless, the company's own internal documents reveal that it and its rivals use ammonia compounds to increase nicotine delivery. A 1991 Brown & Williamson confidential blending manual states:

> "Ammonia, when added to a tobacco blend, reacts with the indigenous nicotine salts and liberates free nicotine. . . . As the result of such change the ratio of extractable nicotine to bound nicotine in the smoke may be altered in favor of extractable nicotine. As we know, extractable nicotine contributes to impact in cigarette smoke and this is how ammonia can act as an impact booster." According to the Brown & Williamson manual, all American cigarette manufacturers except Liggett use ammonia technology in their cigarettes.

145. Tobacco industry patents also show that the cigarette industry has developed the capability to manipulate nicotine levels in cigarettes to an exacting degree. For example:

a. A Philip Morris patent application discusses an invention that "permits the release in controlled amounts and when desired, of nicotine into tobacco smoke."

b. Another Philip Morris patent application explains that the proposed invention "is particularly useful for the maintenance of the proper amount of nicotine in tobacco smoke," and notes that "previous efforts have been made to add nicotine to Tobacco Products when the nicotine level in the tobacco was undesirably low."

c. A 1991 RJR patent application states that "processed tobaccos can be manufactured under conditions suitable to provide products having various nicotine levels."

146. David A. Kessler, MD, Commissioner of the Food and Drug Administration, testified in detail before the Waxman Committee about the various forms of nicotine manipulation practiced by the tobacco industry: manipulating the rate at which nicotine is delivered in the cigarette: transferring nicotine from one material to another; increasing the amount of nicotine in cigarettes; and adding nicotine to any part of a cigarette.

147. Dr. Kessler's disclosures show that nicotine is not an inevitable or unavoidable component of tobacco products. In fact, each of the defendant cigarette manufacturers has the capability to remove all or virtually all of the nicotine from cigarettes using technology already in existence.

148. The cigarette manufacturers' manipulation and control of nicotine levels is further evidenced by the emergence of companies that specialize in manipulating nicotine and that are now offering their services to tobacco manufacturers. On information and belief, a process called tobacco reconstitution, patented and marketed by the Kimberly-Clark Corporation subsidiary, LTR Industries, is widely used throughout the industry.

149. Reconstituted tobacco is made from stalks and stems and other waste that cigarette manufacturers formerly discarded and now used to make cigarettes more cheaply. In the reconstitution process, pieces of tobacco material undergo treatment that results in the extraction of some soluble components, including nicotine. The pieces are then physically formed into a sheet of tobacco material, to which the extracted nicotine is re-added. Although denied by tobacco executives, it is publicly reported that this process adjusts nicotine levels in the products, and that one manufacturer "readily admits to setting levels of nicotine. . . . for the tobacco sheet."

150. An advertisement in tobacco industry trade publications for the Kimberly-Clark tobacco reconstitution process states:

"Nicotine levels are becoming a growing concern to the designers of modern cigarettes, particularly those with lower 'tar' deliveries. The Kimberly-Clark tobacco reconstitution process used by LTR Industries permits adjustments of nicotine to your exact requirements. . . .

We can help you control your tobacco."

151. The tobacco industry's own trade literature explains that the Kimberly-Clark process enables manufacturers to triple or even quadruple the nicotine content of reconstituted tobacco, thereby increasing the nicotine content of the final manufactured product.

152. Another enterprise quite explicitly specializes in the manipulation of nicotine and its use as an additive. This company does business under the name "The Tobacco Companies of the Contraf Group." An advertisement run by the Contraf Group in the international trade press states: "Don't Do Everything Yourself! Let us do it More Efficiently!" Calling itself "The Niche Market Specialists," Contraf lists among its areas of specialization "Pure Nicotine and other special additives."

Light Cigarettes: a Marketing Hoax

153. The cigarette industry's manipulation of nicotine is particularly deceptive in its marketing of "light" or low-tar and low-nicotine cigarettes to retain the health conscious segment of the smoking market. Recent studies demonstrate that cigarettes advertised as low tar and low nicotine have higher concentrations of nicotine, by weight, than high yield cigarettes. Nevertheless, the cigarette manufacturers have successfully identified "light" cigarettes to consumers as a reduced tar and reduced nicotine product. The cigarette manufacturers have accomplished this deception through several strategies.

154. First, cigarette manufacturers have designed their "light" products so that advertised tar and nicotine levels, as measured by the FTC method, understate the amounts of tar and nicotine actually ingested by human smokers. Such design features include a technique called filter ventilation in which nearly invisible holes are drilled in the filter paper, or the filter paper is made more porous. Predictably, many smokers of advertised low tar and nicotine cigarettes block the tiny, laser-generated perforations in ventilated filters with their fingers or lips, thereby resulting in greater tar and nicotine yields to those smokers than those measured by the FTC smoking machine.

155. Cigarette manufacturers know that the ability to block ventilation holes allows smokers to "compensate" for nicotine losses that would otherwise be caused by tar-reducing modifications. The industry has studied smoker compensation in order to design cigarettes that allow smokers to compensate for lower nicotine yields. One such design feature is known as "elasticity." This refers to the ability of a cigarette, whatever its FTC measured nicotine yield, to deliver enough smoke to permit a smoker to obtain the nicotine he needs, e.g., through more or longer puffs, or by covering ventilation holes.

156. Industry studies show that smokers tend to obtain close to the same amount of nicotine from each cigarette despite differences in yield as measured by the FTC smoking machine. In a 1974 BATCO conference, researchers described the result of one such study:

> "The Kippa study in Germany suggests that whatever the characteristics of cigarettes as determined by smoking machines, the smoker adjusts his pattern to deliver his own nicotine requirements (about 0.8 mg. per cigarette)." Smokers' compensation to obtain adequate nicotine also results in the delivery of more tar than the FTC test measure.

157. Second, the FTC testing method does not distinguish between the slower acting salt-bound nicotine and the more potent "free" nicotine that ammonia helps release. An ammoniated cigarette that delivers more potent nicotine to smokers measures the same as a cigarette with no such additives.

158. The use of ammonia is another method used by the cigarette industry to reduce the FTC measured tar and nicotine levels in their cigarettes over the past two decades while still furnishing smokers with sufficient nicotine delivery. According to John Kreisher, a former associate scientific director for CTR, "[a]mmonia helped the industry lower the tar and allowed smokers to get more bang with less nicotine. It solved a couple of problems at the same time."

159. Third, the cigarette industry maintains that nicotine levels follow tar levels. In the words of Dr. Alexander Spears, Vice Chairman of Lorillard, in his 1994 testimony before the Waxman Subcommittee—"[n]icotine [level] follows the tar level," and the correlation between the two "is essentially perfect," and "shows that there is no manipulation of nicotine." Dr. Spears neglected to mention to Congress that in a 1981 study, not intended for public release, he stated explicitly that low-tar cigarettes use special blends of tobacco to keep the level of nicotine up while tar is reduced: "[T]he lowest tar segment [of product categories] is composed of cigarettes utilizing a tobacco blend which is significantly higher in nicotine." RJR, Lorillard, ATC, and TI have similarly represented to the public and to the FDA that the nicotine levels in their products are purely a function of setting the tar levels of such products.

160. ATC told the Waxman Subcommittee in an October 14, 1994 letter that "nicotine follows 'tar' delivery, i.e. high 'tar'-high nicotine, low 'tar'—low nicotine. . . . Nicotine is neither adjusted nor altered to compensate for losses inherent in the manufacturing process." Internal company documents reviewed by the Waxman Subcommittee show, however, that ATC's experimentation with adding nicotine to its tobacco was extensive—extensive enough for ATC executive John T. Ashworth to

instruct employees in a confidential memorandum: "In the future, our use of nicotine should be referred to as 'Compound W' in our experimental work, reports, and memorandums, either for distribution within the Department or for outside distribution."

161. Recent tests conducted at the direction of the FDA show that the low-tar brands actually have more nicotine by weight than the non-"light" brands. The high level of nicotine found in lower tar cigarettes seriously misleads consumers and renders the industry's claim of an "essentially perfect" correlation between reduced tar and nicotine levels false. According to the FDA, this has been accomplished by a combination of the methods described above for boosting nicotine delivery to compensate for nicotine losses from the application of tar-reducing design modifications. The cigarette industry thereby maintains a continuing market for a product that consumers are misled to believe contains less of all of the harmful ingredients in regular cigarettes.

162. Against this mounting body of evidence of the cigarette industry's manipulation and control of nicotine levels in cigarettes, the cigarette manufacturers continue to deny to the public, and recently denied to Congress under oath, that they manipulate and control nicotine levels. Top executives from Philip Morris, RJR, Lorillard, Liggett and Brown & Williamson testified in April 1994 that their respective companies do not manipulate nicotine, add it, independently control it, restore it during the manufacturing process, or otherwise achieve a minimum level of nicotine in their products. Thomas E. Sandefur, Jr., CEO of Brown & Williamson, has admitted that the company controlled nicotine, but in a now familiar refrain, stated that the company did so only for "taste."

163. Thus the cigarette manufacturers' attempt to deceive the public and government officials continues. As recently as April 1994, cigarette manufacturers placed advertisements across the country denying that they believe cigarette smoking is addictive, and misleading the public about whether the cigarette manufacturers deliberately control nicotine levels in their products.

164. An advertisement placed by Philip Morris in newspapers across the country in April 1994, affirmatively represented that Philip Morris does not "manipulate" nicotine levels in its cigarettes, and that "Philip Morris does not believe that cigarette smoking is addictive."

165. RJR placed a similar advertisement in newspapers across the United States in 1994 stating that "we do not increase the level of nicotine in any of our products in order to 'addict' smokers. Instead of increasing the nicotine levels in our products, we have in fact worked hard to decrease 'tar' and nicotine. . . ." RJR's advertisement then touted

its use of "various techniques that help us reduce the 'tar' (and consequently the nicotine) yields of our products."

166. These statements mislead the consuming public because. as alleged above, Philip Morris and RJR use various sophisticated techniques to increase the nicotine content in their cigarettes and the actual nicotine delivery to the smokers.

Sales To Minors

167. In Massachusetts, and across the nation, the overwhelming majority of cigarette use and addiction begins when users are children or teenagers. Eighty-two (82%) percent of daily smokers had their first cigarette before age 18, sixty-two (62%) percent before the age of 16, thirty-eight (38%) percent before the age of 14. Thus, a person who does not begin smoking in childhood or adolescence is unlikely ever to begin. The younger a person begins to smoke, the more likely he or she is to become a heavy smoker. Sixty-seven (67%) percent of children who start smoking in the sixth grade become regular adult smokers and forty-six (46%) percent of teenagers who start smoking in the eleventh grade become regular adult smokers.

168. Smoking at an earlier age increases the risk of lung cancer and other diseases. Studies have shown that lung cancer mortality is highest among adults who began smoking before the age of 15.

169. Although young people frequently believe they will not become addicted to nicotine or become long-term users of tobacco products, they often find themselves unable to quit smoking. Among smokers age 12 to 17 years, a 1992 Gallup survey found that 70% said if they had to do it over again, they would not start smoking and 66` said that they want to quit. Fifty-one percent of the teen smokers surveyed had made a serious effort to stop smoking—but had failed.

170. Cigarette smoking among children and teens is on the rise. A 1995 National Institute of Drug Abuse study found that between 1991 and 1994, the proportional increase in smoking rates was greatest among eighth graders, rising by 30.

171. Cigarettes are among the most promoted consumer products in the United States. The Federal Trade Commission reported to Congress that domestic cigarette advertising and promotional expenditures rose from close to $4 billion in 1990 to more than $6 billion in 1993. Tobacco product brand names, logos, and advertising messages are all-pervasive, appearing on billboards, buses, trains, in magazines and newspapers, on clothing and other goods. The effect is to convey the message to young people that tobacco use is desirable, socially acceptable, safe,

healthy, and prevalent in society. Additionally, young people buy the most heavily advertised cigarette brands, whereas many adults buy more generic or value-based cigarette brands which have little or no image-based advertising. Cigarette manufacturers, knowing that their advertising appeals to young people, continue to use these same marketing techniques to sell their products.

172. A July 1995 report by the California Department of Health Services surveyed tobacco advertisements in or around stores. In looking at almost 6,000 stores, it was found that the total average tobacco advertisements and promotions per store was 25.26. Marlboro was the most frequently advertised and promoted cigarette brand with an average of 10.15 advertisements and promotions per store. Camel was the second most frequently advertised and promoted cigarette brand and had an average of 4.84 advertisements and promotions per store. These two brands were the most frequently advertised and promoted cigarette brands. Not surprisingly, Marlboro, Camel, and Newport, the most heavily advertised brands, are the leading brands smoked by children.

173. This same report also found that stores within 1,000 feet of a school had significantly more tobacco advertising and promotions than stores that were not near schools. Stores near schools were also more likely to have at least one tobacco advertisement placed next to candy or displayed at three feet or below. A significantly higher average number of tobacco advertisements also were found on the exterior of stores located in young neighborhoods—communities in which at least one-third of the population in that zip code were 17 years of age or less.

174. RJR has even identified the stores in proximity to the youth market. RJR's Division Manager for Sales wrote all RJR sales representatives in 1990 regarding the "Young Adult Market" and asked them to identify what stores were in proximity to colleges or high schools. A follow-up letter by the sales division calls for a resubmitted list of Y.A.S. (Young Adult Smoker) accounts using new criteria, focusing on all accounts located across from, adjacent to, or in the general vicinity of high schools or college campuses.

175. Despite these disturbing statistics, each of the cigarette manufacturers maintains that the effect of its pervasive advertising and promotion of cigarettes is limited to maintaining brand loyalty and that it has no role in encouraging adolescents to experiment with smoking.

176. The cigarette manufacturers know that they attract underage consumers to their products. For example, since 1988, RJR has used a cartoon character called Joe Camel in its advertising campaign. It has massively disseminated products such as matchbooks, signs, clothing, mugs, and drink can holders advertising Camel cigarettes. The advertis-

ing has been effective in attracting adolescents, and RJR has knowledge of this fact but still continues the Joe Camel advertising campaign. As a result of the campaign, the number of teenage smokers who smoke Camel cigarettes has risen dramatically. One study found that Joe Camel is almost as familiar to six-year old children as Mickey Mouse, is enticing thousands of teens to smoke that brand, and has caused Camel's popularity with 12-17 year olds to surge dramatically. RJR knew or willfully disregarded the fact that cartoon characters attract children.

177. The model who portrayed the "Winston Man" for RJR's Winston brand cigarettes testified before Congress: "I was clearly told that young people were the market that we were going after." He further testified "it was made clear to us that this image was important because kids like to role play, and we were to provide the attractive role models for them to follow. . . . I was told I was a live version of the GI Joe. . . ."

178. An RJR affiliate studied in detail the motivations of young smokers. A "Youth Target" study was the first of a planned series of research studies into the lifestyles and value systems of young men and women in the 15-24 age range, the stated purpose of which was to "provide marketers and policy makers with an enriched understanding of the mores and motives of this important emerging adult segment which can be applied to better decision making in regard to products and programs directed at youth." The study focused on the "primary elements of lifestyles and values among the youth of today," in learning how to market products to children and teens.

Sale of Defective and Unreasonably Dangerous Products

179. The cigarette manufacturers' products are designed, manufactured, marketed, sold and distributed by defendants to be smoked by the consuming public of Massachusetts.

180. The defendants collectively sold or distributed, or aided and abetted in the sale or distribution, of cigarettes containing disease-causing ingredients and nicotine in addictive amounts, which cigarettes were and are defective and unreasonably dangerous.

181. At all relevant times, defendants knew or should have known that smoking their cigarettes is hazardous to human health, causes human disease and is addictive.

182. The cigarette manufacturers and their trade associations, through their funding and control of various studies on the effects of smoking on human health, their control over trade publications, advertising, marketing, and/or through other agreements, understandings and joint ventures and enterprises, conspired with, cooperated with, and/or ren-

dered substantial assistance to each other in the wrongful suppression, active concealment and misrepresentation of material information concerning the facts about the addictiveness of smoking and its role in human disease, to the public at large, constituting a public misrepresentation and a fraud on the marketplace, all to the detriment of the public health, safety and welfare, and thereby causing harm to the Commonwealth of Massachusetts.

183. Cigarettes are an inherently, abnormally, and unreasonably dangerous product. The health risks and costs of cigarette smoking to the citizens of Massachusetts and to the State greatly outweigh any utility that defendants could conceivably claim for their cigarettes. Defendants knew or should have known of the dangers inherent in the use of their product by citizens of Massachusetts, and that those citizens and the Commonwealth itself would be harmed by the foreseeable and intended use of their cigarettes.

COUNT I—UNDERTAKING OF SPECIAL DUTY (Against all defendants except distributor defendants)

184. The Commonwealth restates and incorporates herein the foregoing paragraphs 1-183 of its Complaint.

185. Defendants represented that they would undertake a special responsibility and duty to citizens of the Commonwealth of Massachusetts, and those who advance and protect the public health, including the Department of Medical Assistance, to accept an interest in the public's health as a basic and paramount responsibility; to cooperate closely with those who safeguard the public health; to aid and assist the research effort into all aspects of tobacco use and human health; to continue to research and otherwise undertake all possible efforts to learn all the facts and to discover the truth about smoking and health; and finally, to disclose to the Commonwealth of Massachusetts and its citizens complete and accurate information about the effects of cigarette smoking on human health.

186. Defendants undertook to render such services recognizing that they were necessary for the protection of the public health, including the health of millions of Massachusetts citizens.

187. Defendants have breached and continue to breach their special responsibility and duty by failing to exercise reasonable care to protect their undertaking. Defendants' failure to use due care in performing the duty that they voluntarily undertook to perform has increased the risk of harm to the public and the cost of health care for the Commonwealth of Massachusetts above and beyond what it would have been had de-

fendants not publicly represented that they were going to engage in the undertaking at all.

188. As a direct and proximate result of defendants' conduct, the Commonwealth has suffered and will continue to suffer substantial injuries and damages for which the Commonwealth is entitled to recovery.

COUNT II—BREACH OF WARRANTY

189. The Commonwealth restates and incorporates herein the foregoing paragraphs 1-188 of its Complaint.

190. Defendants have been engaged for many years in the business, or have aided and abetted in the business, of manufacturing, testing, designing, advertising, marketing, packaging, selling, distri-buting, and placing into the stream of commerce in and into Massachusetts their tobacco products, including various brands of cigarettes.

191. Defendants' tobacco products reach Massachusetts users and consumers in substantially the same condition they are in when originally manufactured, distributed and sold by defendants. Defendants have delivered their tobacco products to the residents of Massachusetts in a defective condition, unreasonably dangerous to users and consumers. Defendants expect and intend for their tobacco products to be used by residents of Massachusetts without substantial change affecting the unreasonably dangerous condition.

192. Safer alternative designs have been technologically and economically feasible and known to defendants for years, but defendants have failed to implement them and, in fact, have deliberately suppressed and concealed their research on and development of safer alternative designs.

193. In breaching their duties to plaintiff, defendants have acted intentionally, recklessly, maliciously and wantonly in that each defendant knew or should have known through information exclusively within their control that their cigarettes were defective and unreasonably dangerous if used in the manner intended by defendants. Defendants also knew or should have known that their breach of duty would be substantially certain to result in the injuries complained of herein.

194. The defective condition of defendants' tobacco products directly and proximately caused thousands of Massachusetts citizens to suffer various tobacco-induced diseases, injuries and sicknesses, and directly and proximately caused the Commonwealth of Massachusetts to expend millions of dollars to provide necessary medical and health care to such citizens, thereby causing damage to Massachusetts.

195. Defendants, jointly and severally, expressly and impliedly warranted that their products were safe, of merchantable quality and fit for their intended uses. Defendants breached their warranties because their products were unsafe, were not of merchantable quality and were unfit for their intended uses. Defendants are on notice of these breaches of warranties.

196. As a direct and proximate result of defendants' conduct, the Commonwealth has suffered and will continue to suffer substantial injuries and damages for which the Commonwealth is entitled to recovery.

COUNT III—CONSPIRACY AND CONCERT OF ACTION (Against all defendants except distributor defendants)

197. The Commonwealth restates and incorporates herein the foregoing paragraphs 1-196 of its Complaint.

198. At least as early as the 1950's, defendants entered into an agreement for the unlawful purposes of suppressing and concealing material scientific and medical information concerning smoking, addiction and diseases; representing falsely to the public at various times that they would undertake a special responsibility and duty to citizens of the Commonwealth of Massachusetts to undertake all possible efforts to learn all the facts and to discover and disclose the truth about smoking and health; and of keeping the public ignorant of the defective and unreasonably dangerous condition of cigarettes.

199. Defendants agreed to act jointly and to cooperate with each other in this conspiracy in order to seek to mislead the public. This deception would not have been possible for each cigarette manufacturer acting individually. Through their combined actions of misrepresentation and concealment over the last four decades, defendants have managed to control the material information concerning smoking and health and thereby ensure, through joint misrepresentations and concealment, that the public remains ignorant of the true facts about smoking and health.

200. In furtherance of their conspiracy, the cigarette manufacturers formed the Tobacco Industry Research Council, its successor Council for Tobacco Research, and the Tobacco Institute, whose true purpose was not to discover and disclose the facts about smoking and health, but falsely to gain the public's confidence so that the cigarette manufacturers could suppress and conceal those facts more effectively.

201. The TIRC, CTR and TI actively participated in the conspiracy to conceal, suppress and diffuse all information about the hazards of cigarette smoking.

202. In furtherance of defendants' conspiracy, they also restrained and suppressed research, development, production and marketing of safer cigarettes. Defendants, in furtherance of their conspiracy, gave encouragement and substantial assistance to each other and otherwise aided and abetted each other in perpetrating these wrongful acts.

203. As a direct and proximate result of defendants' unlawful conspiracy, the Commonwealth has suffered and will continue to suffer substantial injuries and damages.

204. As a result of defendants' unlawful conspiracy, defendants are vicariously and jointly and severally liable as to each cause of action alleged in this Complaint.

205. As a direct and proximate result of defendants' conduct, the Commonwealth has suffered and will continue to suffer substantial injuries and damages for which the Commonwealth is entitled to recovery.

COUNT IV—RESTITUTION (Against all defendants except distributor defendants)

206. The Commonwealth restates and incorporates herein the foregoing paragraphs 1-205 of its Complaint.

207. Defendants assumed and owe a duty to pay for the harm caused by their wrongful conduct, yet have repeatedly refused to do so. Instead, defendants have engaged in a conspiracy of suppression, concealment, and deceit in order to deny responsibility and avoid paying for the consequences of the harm they have caused the Commonwealth of Massachusetts and its citizens.

208. Plaintiff has been and is required by statute and contractual obligations to expend substantial sums of money to pay for the harm caused by the wrongful conduct of defendants. Plaintiff intends to charge and recoup from defendants these sums of money Plaintiff's expenditures are immediately necessary to protect the public health and safety.

209. As a result of defendants' wrongful activities, plaintiff has borne a duty that, in law, equity and fairness, ought to have been borne by defendants.

210. As a direct and proximate result of defendants' conduct, the Commonwealth has suffered and will continue to suffer substantial injuries and damages for which the Commonwealth is entitled to recovery.

COUNT V—UNJUST ENRICHMENT

211. The Commonwealth restates and incorporates herein the foregoing paragraphs 1-210 of its Complaint.

212. Defendants, through their wrongful conduct as described in this Complaint, have reaped substantial profits from the sale of cigarettes in Massachusetts. These cigarette sales, in turn, have resulted in enormous increases in health care costs directly attributable to cigarette smoking.

213. Without justification, defendants have refused and failed to pay for the consequences of their unlawful conduct. The Commonwealth's expenditure of substantial sums to pay for the costs of medical care for indigent smokers has unjustly enriched the defendants.

214. As a result, plaintiff has been required to pay for the medical costs resulting from defendants' unlawful conduct. Plaintiff has borne a duty that, in law, equity and fairness, ought to have been borne by defendants.

215. In equity and good conscience, it would be unjust for defendants to enrich themselves at the expense of plaintiff.

216. As a direct and proximate result of defendants' conduct, the Commonwealth has suffered and will continue to suffer substantial injuries and damages for which the Commonwealth is entitled to recovery.

RELIEF REQUESTED

WHEREFORE, the Commonwealth requests that this Honorable Court issue an order and judgment against the defendants, jointly and severally, as follows:

A. Ordering defendants to disclose, disseminate, and publish all research previously conducted directly or indirectly by themselves and their respective agents, affiliates, servants, officers, directors. employees, and all persons acting in concert with them, that relates to the issue of smoking and health and addiction;

B. Ordering defendants to fund a corrective public education campaign relating to the issue of smoking and health, administered and controlled by an independent third party;

C. Ordering defendants to fund smoking cessation programs including the provision of nicotine replacement therapy for dependent smokers;

D. Ordering defendants to disclose the nicotine yields of their products based on machine tests and human confirmation studies for each brand;

E. Ordering defendants to pay restitution;

F. Awarding damages and compen-sation to the Commonwealth for past and future damages, including but not limited to health care expenditures, caused by the defendants' actions in violation of the laws of the Commonwealth, together with interests and costs;

G. Awarding the Commonwealth reasonable attorney's fees and costs pursuant to St. 1994, c. 60, § 276;

H. Granting such other and further relief as this Court deems equitable and proper.

PLAINTIFF DEMANDS A JURY TRIAL OF ALL CLAIMS SO TRIABLE COMMONWEALTH OF MASSACHUSETTS

[Names and Addresses of Attorneys for Plaintiffs]

APPENDIX 12:
TOBACCO CONTROL LEGISLATION (1998)

MINORS' ACCESS TO TOBACCO PRODUCTS

No retailer may sell cigarettes or smokeless tobacco to any person younger than 18 years of age. For individuals under 27 years of age, retailers shall verify age by means of photographic identification. (FDA regulation, section 897.14)

Section 1926 of the Public Health Service Act requires states to enact legislation restricting the sale and distribution of tobacco products to minors as a condition of receiving federal substance abuse prevention and treatment block grant funds. States are also required to enforce these laws in a manner "that can reasonably be expected to reduce the extent to which tobacco products are available to individuals under the age of 18." (42 USC 300x-26)

Federal agencies must establish regulations to prohibit the sale of tobacco products in vending machines placed in or around any facility maintained, leased or owned by the agency. Regulations also must cover distribution of free samples of tobacco products in or around agency facilities (40 USC 48[c]).

SMOKEFREE INDOOR AIR

Persons that provide children's services funded by the Department of Health and Human Services, the Department of Education, or the Department of Agriculture in indoor facilities (e.g. schools, libraries, day care, health care, and early childhood development settings) are required to prohibit smoking in those facilities if they are regularly or routinely used for the delivery of such services to children. In addition, all Federal agencies that provide such services are also required to prohibit smoking in facilities used regularly or routinely for the delivery of children's services. (20 USC 6081-6084)

Smoking is prohibited on all flights that are no more than 6 hours in duration. (49 USC 41706)

Smoking is prohibited or restricted to separately ventilated areas in Federal facilities (Executive Branch only) (Executive Order 13058)

TOBACCO ADVERTISING

Tobacco advertising is not allowed on television and radio (15 USC 1335). Health warnings are required on advertisements for all tobacco products, except billboards for smokeless tobacco products. (15 USC 1333, 4402)

Federal Preemption: "No requirement or prohibition based on smoking and health shall be imposed under State law with respect to the advertising or promotion of any cigarettes the packages of which are labeled in conformity with the provisions of this chapter." [The Federal Cigarette Labeling and Advertising Act] (15 USC 1334)

GLOSSARY

Abnormal Use—The use of an article in a manner, or for a purpose, other than that which was intended.

Accident—An unforeseen event, occurring without intent or design on the part of the person whose act caused it.

Action—A judicial proceeding whereby one party prosecutes another for a wrong done, for protection of a right, or prevention of a wrong.

Affirmative Defense—In a pleading, a matter constituting a defense.

Aggrieved Party—One who has been injured, suffered a loss, or whose legal rights have been invaded by the act of another.

Allegation—Statement of the issue that the contributing party is prepared to prove.

Alternative Design—The showing that the design of a product was unreasonably dangerous in comparison to a functional design alternative that would have produced a similar benefit with less risk.

American Arbitration Association (AAA)—National organization of arbitrators from whose panel arbitrators are selected for labor and civil disputes.

Answer—In a civil proceeding, the principal pleading on the part of the defendant in response to the plaintiff's complaint.

Appeal—Resort to a higher court for the purpose of obtaining a review of a lower court decision.

Appellant—One who appeals a decision.

Appellee—The party who argues against setting aside an appealed judgment.

Appellate Court—A court having jurisdiction to review the law as applied to a prior determination of the same case.

Arbitration—The reference of a dispute to an impartial person chosen by the parties to the dispute who agree in advance to abide by the arbitrator's award issued after a hearing at which both parties have an opportunity to be heard.

Assumption of Risk—The legal doctrine that a plaintiff may not recover for an injury to which he assents.

Breach of Duty—In a general sense, any violation or omission of a legal or moral duty.

Breach of Warranty—An infraction of an express or implied agreement as to the title, quality, content or condition of a thing which is sold.

Burden of Proof—Duty to substantiate an allegation or issue to avoid dismissal of the issue or to convince the trier of fact of the truth of the claim.

Capacity—Referring to the legal capacity to sue, it is the requirement that a person bringing the lawsuit have a sound mind, be of lawful age, and be under no restraint or legal disability.

Case—An action, cause, suit, controversy, or contested question of law.

Cause of Action—A claim in law and fact sufficient to require judicial attention.

Caveat Emptor—Latin for "Let the buyer beware." A rule of law that the purchaser buys at his or her own risk.

Caveat Venditor—Latin for "Let the seller beware."

Charge—Judicial instructions to a jury.

Citation—A reference to a source of legal authority, such as a statute.

Claim—Assertion of a right.

Claimant—One who makes a claim.

Comparative Negligence—Proportional sharing between plaintiff and defendant of compensation for injuries, based on the relative negligence of both parties.

Compensatory Damages—Those damages directly referable to the tortious act, and which can be readily proven, for which the injured party should be compensated as a matter of right.

Complaint—In a civil proceeding, the first pleading of the plaintiff setting out the facts on which the claim for relief is based.

Component Part—A tangible accessory or constituent unit within a product that is intended to be assembled with other parts into a complete finished product.

Compromise and Settlement—An arrangement arrived at, either in court or out of court, for settling a dispute upon what appears to the parties to be equitable terms.

Conclusion of Fact—Conclusion reached solely through natural reasoning based on facts.

Conclusion of Law—Conclusion reached through application of rules of law.

Consumer Expectation—The expectation of a reasonable consumer as to the safety characteristics, limitations or condition of a product.

Consumer Product—A product intended for individuals to use around a home for personal benefit.

Contingency Fee—The fee charged by an attorney, which is dependent upon a successful outcome in the case, and is often agreed to be a percentage of the party's recovery.

Contribution—Sharing of a loss or payment among two or more parties.

Contributory Negligence—The act or omission amounting to want of ordinary care on the part of the complaining party, which, concurring with the defendant's negligence, is the proximate cause of his or her injury.

Costs—A sum payable by the losing party to the successful party for his or her expenses in prosecuting or defending a case.

Counterclaims—Counterdemands made by a respondent in his or her favor against a claimant. They are not mere answers or denials of the claimant's allegation.

Crashworthiness—The ability of the interior furnishing or design of a vehicle to protect a user from the effects of secondary injury within the vehicle at the time that vehicle collides with another object.

Cross-claim—Claim litigated by co-defendants or co-plaintiffs, against each other, and not against a party on the opposing side of the litigation.

Damages—Monetary compensation which the law awards to one who has been injured by the action of another.

Danger—Unreasonable or unacceptable combination of hazard and risk.

Decedent—One who is deceased, that is, who has ceased to live.

Defective—Lacking an essential; incomplete, deficient, faulty.

Defendant—In a civil proceeding, the party responding to the complaint.

Demonstrative Evidence—Physical evidence which is evidence, contains evidence, or illustrates facts in a controversy.

Deposition—A method of pretrial discovery which consists of a statement of a witness under oath, taken in question and answer form as it would be in court, with opportunity given to the adversary to be present and cross-examine, with all being reported and transcribed stenographically.

Directed Verdict—Decision by the trial court by which the judge determines that a claim or defense has insufficient supporting evidence to let the claim or defense go to the jury for consideration.

Disclaimer—Words or conduct which tend to negate or limit warranty in the sale of goods, which in certain instances must be conspicuous and refer to the specific warranty to be excluded.

Discovery—Modern pretrial procedure by which one party gains information held by another party.

Duty—The obligation, to which the law will give recognition and effect, to conform to a particular standard of conduct toward another.

Expert Testimony—Testimony by an expert witness in relation to a scientific, technical or professional matter.

Expert Witness—Person having special knowledge, wisdom, skill, or information gained by study, investigation, observation, practice or experience relative to the subject matter under consideration.

Express Warranty—A promise by a merchant that goods will have a certain performance, characteristic or content.

Fact Finder—In a judicial or administrative proceeding, the person, or group of persons, that has the responsibility of determining the acts relevant to decide a controversy. It is the role of a jury in a jury trial. In a non-jury trial, the judge sits both as a fact-finder and as the trier of law.

Fact Finding—A process by which parties present their evidence and make their arguments to a neutral person who issues a nonbinding report based on the findings which usually contains a recommendation for settlement.

Fitness—Suitable for the need or use.

Foreseeability—A concept used to limit the liability of a party for the consequences of his acts to consequences that are within the scope of a foreseeable risk.

Foundation—Necessary showing of underlying facts or conditions for admitting exhibits and opinions into evidence.

Fraud—An intentional deception which results in the injury to another.

Hazard—A condition which presents a potential for injury.

Hazardous Substance—Chemicals, finished products, or consumer goods that meet certain definition standards of potential human hazard as found in federal regulations.

Hearing—A proceeding during which evidence is taken for the purpose of determining the facts of a dispute and reaching a decision.

Implied Warranty—A promise about a product's characteristics, safety or performance that while not expressly stated may be implied by law under the Uniform Commercial Code.

Indemnify—To secure against loss or damage that may occur in the future, or to provide compensation for loss or damage already suffered.

Intentional Tort—A tort or wrong perpetrated by one who intends to do that which the law has declared wrong, as contrasted with negligence in which the tortfeasor fails to exercise that degree of care in doing what is otherwise permissible.

Intervening Cause—One of the several events causing harm that, as a matter of law, interrupts the proximate causation of an earlier causal event.

Joint and Several Liability—Two or more parties may be liable to another party for an entire claim even though the parties who are liable are entitled to a proportionate contribution.

Judgment—A final determination of the rights of the contending parties.

Jurisdiction—The power to hear and determine a case.

Label—Information affixed to and/or presented with a product.

Latent Defect—Hidden, concealed or dormant defect which is not discoverable by observation or reasonably careful inspection.

Latent Disease—The appearance of an illness in a person a considerable amount of time after the causal event or exposure.

Lex Loci Delecti—Law of the place where the alleged injury occurred.

Liability—Obligation to do, or refrain from doing, something.

Manufacturing Defect—An unintended aspect of a finished product, due to error or omission in assembly or manufacture, that causes an injury.

Market Share Theory—The legal theory applicable in some jurisdictions when an individual defendant cannot be identified from a class of manufacturers of a specific product, which holds each manufacturer liable according to its percentage of sales in the geographic area where an injury occurs.

Material—In litigation, evidence is material if it relates to the issues.

Misrepresentation—The legal doctrine allocating liability to a defendant that misled users or made false statements concerning the performance or safety of a product.

Misuse—The use of a product contrary to its label directions, instructions, or expected usage.

Motion—An application to the court requesting an order or ruling in favor of the applicant.

Negligence—Negligence is the failure to use such care as a reasonably prudent and careful person would use under similar circumstances.

Negligence Per Se—Conduct, whether of action or omission, which may be declared and treated as negligence without any argument or proof as to the particular surrounding circumstances, either because it is in violation of a statute or valid municipal ordinance, or because it is so palpably opposed to the dictates of common prudence that it can be said without hesitation or doubt that no careful person would have been guilty of it.

Nominal Damages—A trivial sum of money which is awarded as recognition that a legal injury was sustained, although slight.

Patent Defect—A plainly visible defect or one that can be discovered by inspection exercising ordinary care.

Peremptory Challenge—The process of striking a juror from a panel during the voir dire examination without explanation or justification.

Perjury—Willful and corrupt sworn statement made without sincere belief in its truth in a judicial proceeding regarding a material matter.

Plaintiff—In a civil proceeding, the one who initially brings the lawsuit.

Pleadings—Statements, in legal form, setting forth the facts that constitute the plaintiff's cause of action and the defendant's ground of defense.

Precedent—A previously decided case which is recognized as authority for the disposition of future cases.

Prima Facie Case—A case which is sufficient on its face, being supported by at least the requisite minimum of evidence, and being free from palpable defects. A prima facie case is one which will usually prevail in the absence of contradictory evidence.

Privity of Contract—The relationship that exists between two or more contracting parties.

Product Liability—The legal liability of manufacturers and sellers to compensate buyers, users, and even bystanders, for damages or injuries suffered because of defects in goods purchased.

Proximate Cause—That which, in a natural and continuous sequence, unbroken by any efficient intervening cause, produces injury, and without which the result would not have occurred.

Punitive Damages—Compensation in excess of compensatory damages which serve as a form of punishment to the wrongdoer who has exhibited malicious and willful misconduct.

Recall—The withdrawal of a marketed product from sale.

Res Ipsa Loquitur—Literally, "the thing speaks for itself." Res ipsa loquitur refers to the rule of evidence whereby negligence of an alleged wrongdoer may be inferred from the mere fact that the accident happened, provided that the character of the accident and circumstances surrounding it lead reasonably to the belief that in the absence of negligence, it would not have occurred, and that thing which caused the injury is shown to have been under the management and control of the alleged wrongdoer.

Restatement of the Law—A series of volumes authored by the American Law Institute that tell what the law in a general area is, how it is changing, and what direction the authors think this change should take, for example, the Restatement of the Law of Torts.

Retainer Agreement—A contract between an attorney and the client stating the nature of the services to be rendered and the cost of the services.

Risk—Exposure to injury or loss.

Risk/Benefit Analysis—A test of defectiveness which weighs the benefits of a product against its safety risks.

Settlement—A compromise achieved by the adverse parties in a civil suit before final judgment, whereby they agree between themselves upon their respective rights and obligations, thus eliminating the necessity of a judicial resolution of the controversy.

State of the Art—The legal measurement that compares the defendant's product to the most safe of the functional alternative brands of similar products.

Statute of Limitations—Any law which fixes the time within which parties must take judicial action to enforce rights or else be thereafter barred from enforcing them.

Strict Liability—A concept applied by the courts in product liability cases, in which a seller is liable for any and all defective or hazardous products which unduly threaten a consumer's personal safety.

Subsequent Remedial Measures Exclusion—The evidentiary rule that prohibits use in evidence of manufacturer activities that occur after the accident.

Summons—A mandate requiring the appearance of the defendant in an action under penalty of having judgment entered against him for failure to do so.

Superseding Cause—A causal event that leads to harm, that occurs after another causal event, and which is so significant that it exceeds the earlier event in its legal consequence so as to become the proximate cause of the harm.

Survival Statute—A statute that preserves for a decedent's estate a cause of action for infliction of pain and suffering and related damages suffered up to the moment of death.

Tort—A private or civil wrong or injury, other than breach of contract, for which the court will provide a remedy in the form of an action for damages.

Tortfeasor—A wrong-doer. One who commits or is guilty of a tort.

Tortious Conduct—Wrongful conduct, whether of act or omission, of such a character as to subject the actor to liability under the law of Torts.

Toxic Tort—An environmental-related injury stemming from exposure to hazardous chemicals.

Transcript—An official and certified copy of what transpired in court or at an out-of-court deposition.

Trial—A judicial examination of issues between parties, whether they are issues of law or of fact, before a court that has jurisdiction over the cause.

Unavoidably Unsafe—A special category of products, such as prescription drugs, which provide such a benefit to society that the products are excluded from strict liability doctrines, if properly manufactured and labeled.

Unconscionable—Refers to a bargain so one-sided as to amount to an absence of meaningful choice on the part of one of the parties, together with terms which are unreasonably favorable to the other party.

Unreasonably Dangerous—The determination by a jury in evaluating a product that has a defect of whether the danger exceeded reasonable norms.

Useful Life—The period of anticipated service of a product after which the product is not expected to continue to perform effectively.

Verdict—The definitive answer given by the jury to the court concerning the matters of fact committed to the jury for their deliberation and determination.

Waiver—Intentional and voluntary surrender of some known right.

Wanton Negligence—Heedless and reckless disregard for another's rights with the knowledge that the act or omission may result in injury or loss to the other.

Warning—A communication informing the product user of potential hazards and directing certain precautions.

Warranty—Statement or representation made by the seller regarding the character or quality of an article sold.

Willful—An act that is intentional, knowing or voluntary.

Wrongful Death Statute—A statute that creates a cause of action for any wrongful act, neglect, or default that causes death. The action is usually brought by the executor or administrator of the decedent's estate, or by his or her surviving family, and is intended to compensate the family for the loss of the economic benefit that it would have received in the form of support, services, or contributions had the decedent lived.

BIBLIOGRAPHY AND ADDITIONAL READING

Black's Law Dictionary, Fifth Edition. St. Paul, MN: West Publishing Company, 1979.

Centers for Disease Control and Prevention (Date Visited: October 2001) <http://www.cdc.gov/>.

Consumer Sentinel (Date Visited: September 2001) <http://www.consumer.gov/sentinel/>.

Federal Trade Commission (Date Visited: September 2001) <http://www.ftc/gov/>.

Gifis, Steven H., *Barron's Law Dictionary, Second Edition*. Woodbury, NY: Barron's Educational Series, Inc., 1984.

National Institute of Standards and Technology (Date Visited: October 2001) <http://www.nist.gov/>.

National Institutes of Health (Date Visited: October 2001) <http://www.nih.gov/>.

National Safety Council (Date Visited: October 2001) <http://www.nsc.org/>.

National Toxicology Program (Date Visited: October 2001) <http://ntp-server.niehs.nih.gov/>.

O'Reilly, James T. and Cody, Nancy C., The Products Liability Resource Manual. Chicago, IL: American Bar Association, 1993.

Product Safety and Liability Reporter (Date Visited: October 2001) <http://www.bna.com/products/corplaw/pslr.htm/>.

System Safety Society (Date Visited: October 2001) <http://www.system-safety.org/>.

Tobacco Products Litigation Reporter (Date Visited: October 2001) <http://tplr.com/>.

United States Department of Agriculture Economic Research Service (Date Visited: October 2001) <http://www.ers.usda.gov/>.

United States Food and Drug Administration (Date Visited: October 2001) <http://www.fda.gov/>.

United States Consumer Product Safety Commission (Date Visited: October 2001) <http://www.cpsc.gov/>.